THE DISAPPEARANCE OF PERCY FAWCETT

AND OTHER

FAMOUS VANISHINGS

The DISAPPEARANCE of

PERCY FAWCETT

AND OTHER

FAMOUS VANISHINGS

By

JANE CLAPP

FOREWORD BY EVAN ANDREWS

Racehorse Publishing

First published in 1961 by Scarecrow Press

First Racehorse Publishing Edition 2017

All rights to any and all materials in copyright owned by the publisher are strictly reserved by the publisher.

Foreword © 2017 Evan Andrews

Racehorse Publishing books may be purchased in bulk at special discounts for sales promotion, corporate gifts, fund-raising, or educational purposes. Special editions can also be created to specifications. For details, contact the Special Sales Department, Skyhorse Publishing, 307 West 36th Street, 11th Floor, New York, NY 10018 or info@skyhorsepublishing.com.

Racehorse Publishing™ is a pending trademark of Skyhorse Publishing, Inc.®, a Delaware corporation.

Visit our website at www.skyhorsepublishing.com.

10 9 8 7 6 5 4 3 2 1

Library of Congress Cataloging-in-Publication Data is available on file.

Cover photographs: Shutterstock and Pixabay

Print ISBN: 978-1-63158-181-6
Ebook ISBN: 978-1-63158-182-3

Printed in the United States

CONTENTS

NOTE

These ten accounts of famous disappearances have been assembled to present significant facts and plausible theories regarding each disappearance. The reports can claim neither to uncover new evidence, nor to offer original solutions to long-standing mysteries. With few exceptions, no primary sources were examined for overlooked clues. However, available information, as given in books, magazines and newspapers, has been reviewed, and the findings presented as a "first reader" in unresolved disappearances. In several instances, popular belief is at odds with the official accounts of why and how these people vanished. Examples of a process by which imagination takes the grain of fact and produces the pearl of legend are seen in the current solutions to the mystery of Amelia Earhart — Commander Crabb — and Judge Crater.

Perhaps some reader will see a pattern or design in these reports that will enable final solution of one or more of the puzzles.

PICTURE SOURCE CREDITS

Credit is acknowledged and appreciation expressed for use of photographs, and other pictures, to the following individuals and organizations:

FOREWORD

In 1925, the British explorer Colonel Percy Fawcett planned to strike out into the Brazilian jungle on what was supposed to be his last and most triumphant expedition. The fifty-seven-year-old was a born adventurer—his exploits are often cited as an inspiration for the Indiana Jones character—but he was also a man driven by a tantalizing obsession. During his previous journeys into the bush, he had become convinced that an ancient, undiscovered metropolis lay somewhere in the heart of the Amazon. Desperate to find this lost city, which he called "Z," Fawcett scraped together funding and outfitted a small team that included his son Jack and another young man named Raleigh Rimell. That May, the trio set off into Brazil's uncharted Mato Grosso region, intent on making what Fawcett promised would be "the great discovery of the century."

Neither Colonel Fawcett nor his two young companions were ever seen again. It was three years before the first rescue party left to search for them, and since then there have been dozens of other would-be relief missions, many of which have ended in disaster and death. It's now estimated that as many as one hundred people have either been killed or vanished while looking for Fawcett. In 1996, a Brazilian team was captured and held for ransom by Amazonian Indians while questing for information on his fate.

Percy Fawcett's case remains unexplained to this day. What little evidence there is suggests he met his end at the hands of hostile native Indians, but he just as easily might have perished from tropical disease, starvation, or an animal attack. Perhaps he somehow found his mythical city of Z and chose to live out his days in the jungle. Like all great disappearances, the possibilities are endless and the answers perpetually out of reach.

--> --> --> -->

As a history writer, I've always been fascinated by stories like Fawcett's. There's something irresistible about the blank spots of the past—those incidents that remain stubbornly mysterious no matter how much we try to research or resolve them. With this in mind, I was immediately drawn in by Jane Clapp's *The Disappearance of Percy Fawcett and Other Famous Vanishings*. In these brief sketches, the author presents ten tales of missing persons, each one of them drenched in human drama, intrigue, and enigma. It's easy to veer off into crackpot territory when discussing these kinds of stories, but Clapp has an even hand and an open mind. Rather than endorsing pet theories or engaging in idle speculation, she focuses her commentary on what she calls "significant facts and plausible theories." Think of her book as a detective's notes on some of history's coldest cold cases.

Several "greatest hits" are on display, from Ambrose Bierce and Amelia Earhart to Joseph Force Crater, the New York judge whose 1930 vanishing grabbed so many headlines that the phrase "Pulling a Crater" became slang for a disappearing act. Yet Clapp also touches on some of the lesser-known missing persons of the past. Many readers may have never before heard the story of Jesus de Galindez, a political activist and Columbia University professor who vanished in New York, possibly on the orders of the infamous Dominican dictator

Rafael Trujillo. Another unsung case is that of Charley Ross, a four-year-old Philadelphia boy whose 1874 abduction was one of the United States' first high profile child kidnappings. Ross, who was lured from his home by men who promised him sweets and firecrackers, is now cited as the inspiration for a classic parental warning: "Never take candy from strangers."

The figures Clapp discusses went missing under a variety of circumstances, but they tend to share certain common features. Some, such as Percy Fawcett, Amelia Earhart, and Richard Halliburton, were fearless adventurers known for pushing themselves to extremes. They spent their lives exploring the far edges of the map until they finally dropped clear off the edge of it. Clapp encapsulates the wanderlust and derring-do of these people in just a few pages, which only makes the details of their disappearances all the more mystifying.

I was particularly taken with the story of Halliburton, the roving travel writer who vanished in 1939 while trying to sail a Chinese junk from Hong Kong to San Francisco. Halliburton isn't well known today, but in his own time he was a literary celebrity famed for such quixotic stunts as sleeping atop the Great Pyramid of Giza, stranding himself on a deserted island, and swimming the Panama Canal (his thirty-six-cent toll remains the cheapest in the canal's history). Had he lived today, it'd be easy to picture him as a reality TV star or travel show host.

In other cases, the figures covered here disappeared in the haze of political or organized crime-related intrigue. These include Judge Crater, Jesus de Galindez, and Commander Lionel "Buster" Crabb, the British frogman who vanished—and whose body later reappeared, minus its hands and head—while diving near a Soviet warship in 1956. These tales leave behind some of the juiciest unanswered questions. Why did Crater destroy some of his personal papers and withdraw thousands of dollars from his bank account before disappearing? What was the nature of Commander Crabb's diving mission in Portsmouth Harbor? These people were all seemingly involved in some form of plot or conspiracy. They became entangled with forces beyond their control, and it may have gotten them killed.

We often say that vanished people have "disappeared without a trace," but as this book shows, there are always traces, however faint or unreliable. Each of these figures was the subject of a sweeping manhunt, and as time passed, they seemed to materialize wherever rumor and hearsay decided to place them. Throughout the 1930s, Judge Crater was variously spotted lounging on cruise ship decks, praying in a Mexican monastery, and laying low in Italy. Percy Fawcett was claimed to be a bearded South American beggar or a jungle king leading a band of Amazonian cannibals. Ambrose Bierce, the author and satirist who disappeared in Mexico, was identified both as a member of Pancho Villa's army and the victim of one of its firing squads.

In some instances, the missing even reappeared in the form of imposters. For years after the vanishing of Charley Ross, his family faced an endless parade of conmen and inheritance seekers who purported to be the missing boy in the flesh. Stranger still is the case of Sir Roger Tichborne, the young British aristocrat who disappeared at sea in 1854. Over a decade later, a man named Arthur Orton surfaced in Australia claiming he was the vanished heir. Orton looked nothing like Tichborne—for one, he was a full two hundred pounds heavier—but his story became a sensation in Victorian-era Britain. He won legions of supporters, and it ultimately took two court cases before his claims were officially debunked. Such is often the case when it comes to unexplained mysteries. In their quest to find answers, people are often willing to believe anything, no matter how outlandish.

···→ ···→ ···→ ···→

The disappearances Clapp discusses all unfolded during the nineteenth and early twentieth centuries, but many are still being investigated today. Even since this book was first written, new evidence and theories have emerged regarding some of its subjects. One of the most titillating developments concerns Commander Lionel Crabb. The diver's disappearance has long been one of the most mysterious chapters of the Cold War, inspiring everyone from conspiracy theorists to James Bond creator Ian Fleming, who lifted elements of it for his 1961 novel *Thunderball.* It once again made headlines in 2007, when a retired Russian diver named Eduard Koltsov told a documentary crew that he had slit Crabb's throat after catching him trying to plant a mine on the Soviet vessel *Ordzhonikidze.* The story has not been confirmed, but photos from news articles showed Koltsov posing with the dagger he supposedly used to deliver the killing blow. In 2015, meanwhile, the British government finally declassified documents showing that Crabb was part of an ill-planed spying mission.

Another major source of new research is Amelia Earhart, the iconic lady aviator who vanished in 1937 during a round-the-world flight. The most common explanation has always been that Earhart and navigator Fred Noonan ran out of fuel and crashed in the Pacific Ocean while trying to locate Howland Island. In recent years, however, some investigators have argued that the fliers instead made an emergency landing on tiny Gardner Island—now known as Nikumaroro—where they later died as castaways. Since the 1980s, The International Group for Historic Aircraft Recovery, or TIGHAR, has maintained a special "Earhart Project" dedicated to shedding light on the pilot's fate. In 1991, its investigators recovered a sheet of aluminum on Nikumaroro that may have been part of Earhart's Lockheed Electra. Other finds on the island include 1930s-era women's cosmetics, jacket buttons, and possible human bone fragments. The Nikumaroro theory remains unconfirmed, but as recently as 2015, TIGHAR was still conducting new research on the island.

A final area of fresh research involves Colonel Percy Fawcett. The Amazon has kept his fate secret for over ninety years, but recent developments have offered a faint suggestion of how the explorer may have died. In writing his 2009 book *The Lost City of Z*, author David Grann journeyed to the Brazilian jungle and interviewed many of its natives, including members of the Kalapalo tribe. According to Grann, the tribe recounted a decades-old oral history that told of how Fawcett and his companions had paid them a visit before venturing into the territory of a particularly fierce group of natives. The Kalapalos claimed they spotted smoke from explorers' campfires for several days, but it eventually disappeared, which they took as a sign that the men had been murdered.

We may never know what really happened to the likes of Fawcett, Earhart, and the other figures covered in this book, but that's part of why their stories have such an enduring appeal. By reading these tales, we all get to play the part of the armchair investigator. We assemble the evidence, analyze the key characters, and try to piece together the most plausible theory of what might have happened. Clapp proves to be a thoroughly entertaining guide in this regard, and her book is a fine jumping-off point for anyone wanting to learn the details of these cases and possibly unlock their secrets.

As Clapp says in her author's note, there's always a chance that some perceptive reader will spot a fresh pattern of evidence and break one of the cases wide open. Since this book was first written, none of these vanishings has been explained to any satisfying degree. They stand as some of the most beguiling tales that history has to offer, each one a timeless mystery still waiting to be solved.

—Evan Andrews, 2017

Joseph Force Crater

A JUDGE ON THE LAM

On a hot summer night in New York City, Judge Joseph Force Crater stepped into a taxi on West 45th Street, waved goodnight to two dinner companions, and was never seen again. The resulting investigation of his disappearance covered the United States and many foreign countries, and his "jacket" in the Bureau of Missing Persons of the New York City Police Department, File 13595, still marks an open case.

Judge Crater does not fit the picture of a remote white-haired jurist who spends quiet evenings playing chess and reading the *Yale Review*. He was a sporty character well-known on Times Square and Broadway, and some of his best friends were the long-stemmed American beauties who graced the chorus lines and name roles of popular musicals. While other disappearances from the streets of New York have received a certain notoriety (there was Dorothy Arnold who went shopping on December 12, 1910 and never came home; and Jesus de Galindez who vanished in an improbable political shuffle on March 12, 1956), the Crater case received an av-

alanche of publicity — and for good reason. The com-
bination of personal scandals brought to light about the
judge, and the linking of his disappearance with odorous
political corruption in the city's administration makes
him the most famous missing person of that area.

The world-wide tracing of clews followed telephone
tips, letters, personal visits of informants, notes written
on playing cards found in floating bottles. Judge Crater
was seen as the occupant of a neighboring deck chair
on ocean liners; as the quiet resident of a pension in
Italy; as a heavy better at the races; as a monk in a monastery in Mexico; as a visitor to Sing Sing. Although he had
never learned to drive a car, Judge Crater was recognized as the driver of a variety of vehicles by motorists
in many states. No missing man has ever had more
doubles.

On August 6, 1930, when Judge Crater disappeared,
he was forty-one years old. Today, thirty years after his
disappearance, the search for him continues. Do the facts
show that the judge may live a respected citizen in
some community? Was he killed in a roughing-up ad-
ministered by gangster friends of a woman who was
blackmailing him? Did he commit suicide because of the
personal and political scandals that prevented him from
achieving his life-long goal? Was he robbed and murdered by a man he had never seen before? The facts are
these.

In April 1930, less than four months before his disappearance, Joseph Force Crater, relatively unknown
politically, was appointed Justice of the New York State
Supreme Court by Governor Franklin D. Roosevelt. He
was a compromise appointment to the unexpired term
of resigning Judge Proskauer, and in order to secure a
full fourteen-year term as Justice, a political plum paying $22,500 a year, would face election in November

of that year.

Born in a small town, Easton, Pennsylvania, in 1889, and educated in a local school, Lafayette College, in his home town, Joseph Crater had allied himself in New York City with the Tammany Democrats. For over ten years he had acted as President of the Cayuga Democratic Club in the nineteenth district. From 1920 to 1926 he was secretary to State Supreme Court Justice Robert F. Wagner. Judge Crater's legal practice, involving many receiverships, paid well. So well that he had become a heavy and successful speculator in the stock market. One of his several brokers accounts showed a turnover of $120,000. Judge Crater's other professional activities included teaching at Fordham University and at New York University, where he had the academic rank of Assistant Professor and the reputation of the most entertaining lecturer in the law school.

The Judge, according to his wife, the former Stella Mance Wheeler, a slim, attractive blonde, was most punctual in his habits. He always let her know when he would be away from home for dinner, and whenever he would be delayed or absent, he telephoned or sent a telegram. Perhaps he sent such messages rather frequently because he was often seen in the speak easy nightclubs of the era, and in popular restaurants. Judge Crater was described as gregarious. His friends included fellow jurists, politicians, professional men, show men, and show girls. He enjoyed the theater and frequently attended plays and musicals.

But there was something enigmatic about this sociable, friendly man. He often attended the theater alone. He contributed to the maintenance of several women other than his wife. Sylvia Marcus, a pretty red-haired salesgirl, had received an allowance from the Judge for over seven years, and he was a regular visitor to her apartment. Fred Kahler, the Crater chauffeur, testified the Judge's destinations were often vague. He seldom went to any specific address, but left the car at street intersections, and arranged to be picked up on corners rather than at any house or building.

In physical appearance, Judge Crater was tall, of robust build; he had brown eyes, graying hair, parted in the center, his upper and lower teeth had been replaced. An injury in a car door had permanently deformed the end of his right index finger. Although a tall man, he walked with very short steps. Because of his unusually long, thin neck (collar size 14), he wore high white collars. He had a head markedly small for his stature (hat size 6 5/8). The judge was customarily quiet and deliberate in manner, and, although a social drinker in moderation, he was known as a sparing user of alcohol.

The backdrop of politics before which the Crater disappearance and investigation were enacted was a montage of bribery, graft, corrupt practices. The Seabury investigations, shortly to get under way, revealed some of the payoffs that were the order of the day in New York municipal administration. The findings of the investigations, The Seabury Report completed several years after Judge Crater's disappearence, caused Governor Roosevelt to request the resignation of Mayor Jimmie Walker.

Two cases of graft were closely related to the Crater case: The Ewald Investigation, and the Libby's Hotel Scandal. The Ewald payoff came to light when United States Attorney General in New York, Charles P. Tuttle, began a routine check into the activities of the Cotter-Butte Mining Company, which had been charged with using the mails to defraud investors of millions of dollars. Mr. Tuttle uncovered incidental evidence that City Magistrate George F. Ewald had paid $12,000 for his appointment to Martin J. Healy, a leader of the Cayuga Democratic Club, of which Judge Crater was president. Although federal investigators checked the judge's bank accounts, and his father, F. E. Crater, testified he thought his son's disappearance the result of the Ewald investigation, Judge Crater was not proved personally involved in the payoff.

There was some question as to whether the judge, in turn, had paid for his appointment. Several weeks after his appointment was confirmed, he sold securities and withdrew money from the bank to total the approximate amount of his annual salary as Justice — $22,500. A. E. McCabe, a broker, testified that the judge received $16,000 for the stock sold, and that J. L. Mara, the judge's court attendant, called for the cash payment. Judge Crater's regular brokers had no record of the judge selling any of his securities at this time. It is an open political secret that the rule of thumb for pricing such political appointments was "one year's salary." Coincidence might account for the closeness in amount of the judge's annual salary and the cash he secured, which was never accounted for.

The Libby's Hotel Scandal more specifically involves the missing judge. The Libby's Hotel, a substantial brick building on the East Side, was one of the many property receiverships Judge Crater handled in his law practice. On June 27, 1929, the Hotel was sold to the American Mortgage Company, a subsidiary of a New York City finance company, for $75,000. Although the title to the property changed hands, no cash was paid for the Hotel as taxes and other judgments against it were in excess of the purchase price. Less than two months after this sale, the Libby's Hotel was bought by the City of New York for over two and a half million dollars. Purpose: Street widening. The judge's es-

tate received his legally established fee for handling the
property during five months of receivership, some $10,-
000, but an additional "very large sum" the judge noted
was due him when the city purchased the hotel, was denied owing and never paid by the American Mortgage
Company. The street widening project never started,
and when Mayor La Guardia was questioned on the
transaction several years later, he replied, "Page Mr.
Crater."

Several agencies had attempted to do just that, and
for a number of months. The District Attorney of New
York City, and the New York City Police Department
were looking for the missing judge. A Grand Jury
hearing looking into his disappearance called nearly 300
witnesses over a period of four months, and reported
its findings in hundreds of pages of testimony. Mrs.
Crater, aware of political forces in the investigation, said
it was a "burlesque," that politics hampered the police
search, and never testified before the Grand Jury.

The investigations detailed Judge Crater's activities
immediately before his disappearance:

Sunday, August 3, 1930 Judge Crater, vacationing at
his cottage at Belgrade Lakes with Mrs. Crater received a "disturbing" telephone call. He said something to his wife about "having to straighten those
fellows out"; told her he had to return to New York
and would be back at the Lakes Saturday, August
9. Ludwig Traube, his next door neighbor at the
Lakes, telephoned for the judge, as they had an
appointment, and Mrs. Crater told him the judge
had returned to New York "on a very important
matter."

Monday, August 4. Amedia Christian, the Crater's

Puerto Rican maid was told by the judge to return August 7 to clean the apartment. Judge Crater attended to routine business in his chambers, wrote a letter to a niece at a camp in Maine, was seen at lunch in a Broadway restaurant, saw his doctor in Greenwich Village that afternoon.

Tuesday, August 5. Judge Crater was seen in the County courthouse and in his chambers. He had lunch with a fellow jurist, dinner at his physician's where he stayed until 12:30 A.M. On this day, a woman, "Lorraine Fay," was consulting another attorney, S. Rucker, a former Deputy Attorney General of New York State, to file a $100,000 breach of promise against Judge Crater. Lorraine Fay was never identified and never seen again.

Wednesday, August 6. Judge Crater appeared in his office at the usual hour, about 11 A.M. J. L. Mara, his court attendant, was given two checks drawn to cash on local banks and totaling $5150. Judge Crater pocketed the cash Mara handed him without taking it out of the envelope. He called Mara to tie up several portfolios filled with papers from his files, and to carry these and two briefcases to a taxi. When they arrived at the Crater apartment, 40 Fifth Avenue, Mara put the files on chairs in the living room. The judge told him, "I'm going up Westchester way for a swim. I'll see you tomorrow." Mara thought the judge seemed depressed. That evening the judge bought a single ticket for *Dancing Partner*, a new comedy that had just opened the night before at the Belasco Theatre on West 44th Street. Joseph Grainsky, the ticket agent, knew Judge Crater, and told him he would try to locate a ticket for that evening and have it at the boxoffice.

The judge next was seen in Billy Haas' restaurant,
332 West 45th Street, by William Klein, an attorney
who handled legal theatrical work for the Schu-
berts. When he saw Judge Crater, he asked him to
join him and his companion, Sally Lou Ritz, a form-
member of the *Artists and Models* company. The
judge appeared in his usual good spirits during dinner, and told Klein he was returning to Belgrade
Lakes for a three weeks vacation before his court
reconvened on August 25. About 9:15 they came
out of the restaurant. Crater hailed a taxi, waved
as the taxi moved westward on 45th Street — and
vanished.

The ticket he arranged for was picked up at the box-
office, but the person using the ticket was never
identified.

When the judge failed to appear on August 9 at Belgrade Lakes, Mrs. Crater telephoned friends in New
York. She was assured that everything was all right,
and that the judge would be back home in a day or
two. Fred Kahler, the chauffeur, sent by Mrs. Crater to
New York to see whether the judge was at their apartment, telephoned her to report that the apartment was
in good order, but that the judge was not there. All of
the judge's thirty suits, except the brown pin-stripe he
wore the day of his disappearance, hung in the closet.
All the luggage was there. Also, on the dresser, were
the judge's monogrammed watch, card case, and pen,
which he usually carried.

Discreet inquiries were made. Judge Crater's political
friends warned Mrs. Crater that more direct action

would jeopardize the judge's chances for election. Then too, the judge had once before absented himself, for a period of three weeks, and returned safely.

The Supreme Court session began August 25. When Judge Crater had not reported to his chambers by August 27, when he was scheduled to preside at a meeting of the judges, Supreme Court Justice, Louis A. Valentine telephoned Mrs. Crater at Belgrade Lakes to find out where Judge Crater was. On September 3, over a month after the disappearance, the *New York World* reported the story of the missing judge on the front page. The following day, the Bureau of Missing Persons of the New York Police Department received a request to look for the judge. Their famous File 13595 was opened.

Rewards for information were posted. The *Sun* offered $2500; New York City, $5000. The investigation pursued over a period of months cost an estimated $300,000.

There was no trace of Judge Crater. The taxi driver who picked him up in front of Haas' restaurant was not found. "Lorraine Fay," suing for breach of promise, never came forward. A further element of mystery appeared in the case, when Mrs. Crater, upon her return to the Crater apartment on January 21, 1931, found a manila envelope in the top drawer of the dresser. The envelope contained cash, $6690 mostly in bills of large denomination, the judge's 16-line will, written five years before, leaving his entire estate to his wife; insurance policies; securities; and a three page note, pencilled in the judge's handwriting, listing debtors owing him. The Libby's Hotel was listed among the debtors. All debtors denied the obligation and refused payment, with the exception of the receivership fee for the Libby's Hotel. At the bottom of his note, in closing, the judge wrote, "Am very weary. Love, Joe."

The apartment had been thoroughly searched by the

police, by the district attorney, and by Grand Jury investigators. There was 24-hour police guard on the apartment. There was speculation that the envelope had been overlooked in the many searches; that Judge Crater had returned to the apartment after the searches; that the envelope had been placed in the dresser by one of the policemen guarding the apartment. The contents of the envelope are customarily stored in a safety deposit box. When Judge Crater's safety deposit box was opened, he was the only person authorized access to it, the box was empty. When and how the envelope was placed in the apartment were never determined.

July 6 1937, Judge Crater was declared legally dead. Emil K. Ellis, attorney acting for Mrs. Crater, sued the insurance companies carrying the judge's life insurance for double indemnity. Ellis claimed he had proof that Judge Crater was murdered in the vicinity of 39th Street and Park Avenue. He claimed the judge offered the $5120, drawn out of the bank on the day of his disappearance, to a show girl who was trying to blackmail him; was accidently killed in an ensuing scuffle with two strong-arm men; his body taken to New Jersey and cremated under a falsified death certificate. No legal action was taken on the evidence presented, but the insurance companies settled for the face values of the policies, $20,561. Several years ago Mr. Ellis repeated his story to the *Los Angeles Times*. He stated that Judge Crater told friends his life was in danger, and that he had shown them a gun which he carried for protection.

New York District Attorney Crain had tried to find out if Judge Crater's mysterious telephone call that sent him hurrying back to New York from Belgrade Lakes, the day after he arrived for his vacation, told him that he was not going to be nominated for the Supreme Court post.

According to Police Commissoner Edward P. Mulrooney, "Crater's disappearance was premeditated." There are the unexplained papers Judge Crater removed from his files the day he disappeared. There is the finality of leaving his personal papers accessible and in order; his watch, card case, and pen with their identifying initials. There is also the considerable difference in the reported size of the judge's bank and brokerage accounts, and the modest estate he left.

Have you among your friends or acquaintances a tall, distinguished-looking man in his early seventies, who speaks well, and takes an interest in the theater?

Further reading:

Alexander, J. What happened to Judge Crater? *Saturday Evening Post* 233:19-21 September 10, 1960
Bloom, M. T. Is it Judge Crater's body? *Harper's Magazine* 219:41-7 November 1959.
Crater, Stella Force. The empty robe, written with Oscar Fraley.
Manning, George. Most tantalizing disappearance of our time *Colliers* 126: 13-15 July 29, 1950
New York Times 1930-32
Sanger, Joan. The case of the missing corpse.

Lionel Crabb

THE EXPENDABLE FROGMAN

If the International Association of Intelligence Agents and Secret Service Workers has a motto, it is, "Don't get caught." According to an unwritten employer-employee agreement of many years standing, a spy is considered expendable, and if he is caught, he can expect no acknowledgement, let alone help, from the government that pays him. Furthermore, by this serious, and usually fatal, blunder he has embarrassed all governments, groups and agencies that might be remotely connected with his activities. No clearer contemporary example of these truisms can be found than in the case of Commander Lionel Philip Kenneth Crabb, Britain's missing frogman.

For three days in the spring of 1956, April 17 to April 19, Commander Crabb, a pioneer and twice-decorated hero in England's underwater work in World War II, was planning and taking a "dip," for one reason or another, in Portsmouth Harbor. This fact in itself would probably have not been of unusual importance. But the coincidence that the Soviet's light cruiser, Ordzhonikidze,

13

with two attendant destroyers, was anchored at Portsmouth, plus the disappearance of Commander Crabb, placed his last dive in the headlines of the world's press, and resulted in the exchange of stiff notes and announcements by the agencies of the Soviet Union, Great Britain, and the United States.

Rumors and theories concerning Commander Crabb's disappearance are many. He had died when his equipment fouled. He had been killed by a secret weapon on the bottoms of the Russian ships. The Russian frogmen, observed near the ships when they first anchored, had captured him, and, under a truth drug, he had disclosed all the secrets of the Royal Navy. He had been taken to an internment camp in Russia. Are these speculations about Crabb's fate answered, or only multiplied, by the finding of a headless and handless body, in frogman's gear, some miles from Portsmouth the following year?

What was Commander Crabb looking for? Was he checking the hulls of the Soviet ships for mines that might have been attached by anti-Communist groups in England? Was he observing asdic (submarine-detecting sonar) apparatus underneath the Ordzhonikidze? Was he photographing the propeller set, the size and shape of the twin screws, and the rudder to show what made the Russian cruiser faster and more maneuverable than English ships of the same class? Was this just a routine reconnaissance, similar to that made by the Soviet frogman who inspected the British squadron on its visit to Leningrad early in 1956, or that Crabb followed in checking the Sverdlov, a Soviet cruiser visiting Portsmouth some months previously? Was he on the harmless assignment of testing new underwater equipment for the training center in Portsmouth?

Who employed the Commander for this final "dip?" Was it the British Admiralty, or some top-secret intelligence agency of the British government? Was it some group in England outside the government? Was it the United States Navy, or the agency of some other government? Was this assignment volunteered by Commander Crabb on his own initiative, to do well what he knew best?

These are the questions raised when the disappearance was made public. Are there answers to this "mystery of the deep?"

When Lionel Philip Kenneth Crabb first went underwater for the Royal Navy at Gibralter, his diving gear was inadequate by any standards. It inclued such articles as weighted tennis shoes. His assignment was to remove mines from the hulls of British ships, and he was competing in this war exercise with Italian divers, who had the edge in training and gear. He liked the element of danger in submerging, searching for mines, removing delayed-action limpet mines and other explosive devices, possibly booby trapped, and in detonating or disarming mines and bombs. Lionel Crabb performed his duties with ingenuity, intelligence and courage. He left Navy work, in 1955 after his post-war recall to the Navy ended, with the rank of Lieutenant Commander, and decorations including the George Medal, and the Order of the British Empire.

In peacetime work, "Buster," or "Crabbie" Crabb found various bread and butter employments. Before the war his work activities had been varied: merchant marine apprentice, service station attendant in Windgap, Pennsylvania, advertising salesman, and art gallery curator. Commander Crabb's post-war endeavors showed some of this same casualness. Aside from trying to promote the peacetime use of underwater shallow diving, he did apply his wartime experience in short periods of civilian work as underwater photographer, technical ad-

viser for a motion picture about diving, observer for the
Fisheries Bureau. From time to time, he was given special Navy jobs: mine disposal, determining whether there
were any survivors in a disabled submerged submarine,
recovery of secret equipment lost underwater.

In April 1956, he spoke of certain "underwater business," and mentioned "a little job," that took him from
his regular occupation of selling furniture in London, to
Portsmouth. Mrs. Pat Rose, a long-time friend of "Crabbie," Marshall Pugh, who was writing a biography of
the Commander, and Crabb's employer, Mr. Maitland
Pendock, knew he had some assignment in Portsmouth
that caused him some anxiety over equipment. Mrs.
Crabb, the seventy-six year old mother of the Commander, received a letter from her son telling her of his
mission in Portsmouth, and asking her not to worry and
to destroy the letter. About this time in the regular
course of his furniture selling, Crabb sold coffee tables
to a "Bernard S. Smith." Mr. Pendock was under the
impression that Crabb knew Smith and had at one time
worked with him. When the check Smith gave in payment for his purchase was seen to be misdated 1955, instead of 1956, Crabb said he would have Smith correct
this error when he saw him in Portsmouth.

On Tuesday, April 17, the day before the Russian
cruiser, Ordzhonikidze, and her accompanying destroyers anchored at Portsmouth Harbor bringing Marshal
Bulganin and Chairman Khrushchev to visit in England,
Commander Crabb checked in to the Sallyport Hotel,
near the harbor, in Portsmouth. With him was "Mr.
Smith," a tall, fair-haired man of about forty years of
age.

When Crabb called his London employer the next
day, he seemed in good spirits and commented, "Well,
I'm not as old as I thought." This remark was later as-

sumed to mean that Crabb had taken a trial dive and
found that, in spite of his age, he was forty-six, and his
long periods out of the water, he had not lost his diving
skill.

That Wednesday evening Crabb had a reunion with
wartime friends — a petty officer, and a lieutenant commander and his wife. They arranged to meet again on
Thursday, April 19. Crabb was not seen again. On April
19. "Mr. Smith" appeared at the Sallyport Hotel, paid
the account for his and Crabb's accommodations, and
took away their belongings.

Crabb's employer telephoned the commander friend
Crabb had seen on the evening of April 18 to inquire
about him. When the Commander asked several careful
questions of the Navy, he was told not to discuss the matter and to avoid talking further with Crabb's employer.
It was six days after Crabb's disappearance on April 19,
that a navy captain telephoned Mr. Pendock and asked
him to call on him. The officer told him that Crabb had
disappeared in underwater tests in Portsmouth harbor. He secured the address of Crabb's mother. The
following day, when Marshall Pugh telephoned the Admiralty, he too was asked to visit the captain, and was
given the same information. In addition, the captain suggested that Commander Crabb might have been picked
up by a trawler, but he agreed, as both men knew the
commander to be a weak surface swimmer, that he was
probably dead.

In the next several days, after Crabb's mother was
notified of his disappearance, a statement to the press
was made available at the Admiralty, not issued as is
usual. It reported that Commander Crabb was missing
and presumed dead after failing to return from a dive
testing underwater apparatus. The scene of the dive was
first given as in "the Portsmouth area." A later dispatch

changed the location of the dive to "Stokes Bay," several miles from the Russian ships' berth. Reporters were told that the original statement was no longer available.

Immediately after Crabb's disappearance and later when the fact that he was missing became publicly known, there was no known attempt to recover his body.

An additional veil obscured the disappearance when police officials removed several pages from the Sallyport Hotel register. These pages recorded the stay of Commander Crabb and "Mr. Smith." Requests for information concerning this action were stopped by reference to the Official Secrets Act.

The Smith check, that Commander Crabb had intended to clear up in Portsmouth, was paid by a woman, with a Swedish or German accent, who paid the exact amount of the bill at the London furniture store. A higher amount, five pounds, had been carried in the papers as the amount due. This woman eluded questioners. The naval attache at the Soviet Embassy in London stated that a single diver had been observed by Russian seamen near the ships at 7:30 in the morning on April 19. He surfaced briefly between the cruisers, submerged quickly and was not sighted again.

The appearance of this frogman was informally protested by the Russian Admiral, V. F. Kotov, to the Portsmouth Naval Base Commander, Rear Admiral Philip W. Burnett. Admiral Burnett denied the possibility of any frogmen being in the water, pointing out that the underwater training unit in Portsmouth was temporarily inactive.

According to Marshall Pugh, Crabb's biographer, the Commander's colleagues in underwater work thought he was working for a military intelligence agency in examining the Soviet ships. He dived alone, knowing the risk of working without a "dicky," the second diver usually assigned in such dangerous "dips" below the oxygen mask safety level of thirty-three feet. Crabb died of oxygen poisoning.

Mrs. Crabb was brought the effects her son left in the Sallyport Hotel by the same navy captain who had talked with Mr. Pendock and Marshall Pugh. The Navy denied that any gear had been issued Crabb for the dive. Certain problems in Britain's domestic politics were created by the disappearance. During the Soviet officials' visit in England, there were charges of rudeness to the visitors. In particular, the press objected to the treatment given them at a labor official's dinner. It might have been expected that Laborite Mr. Hugh Gaitskill, Leader of the Opposition, would demand an explanation of Commander Crabb's disappearance from the Prime Minister Sir Anthony Eden. Such an incident of espionage could only be considered an even greater rudeness on the part of the Conservatives, and they would be in no position to censure the labor opposition for endangering the government's relations with the Soviet visitors.

The Prime Minister made a formal statement in the House on May 4, two weeks after the frogman was missing:

"It would not be in the public interest to disclose the circumstances in which Commander Crabb is presumed to have met his death. While it is the practice for the Ministers to accept responsibility, I think it is necessary in the special circumstances of the case, to make it clear that what was done was done without the authority or the knowledge of her Majesty's Ministers. Appropriate disciplinary steps are being taken."

At the international level, the Russian press reported

the "shameful espionage," and Soviet notes objected to this open spying on the Russian ships. "Mr. Smith," who had later vanished as completely as had Crabb, the Russians identified as a representative of the United States Navy. In answer, the Navy announced:

"No American personnel were with Crabb at that time. We know nothing of the case."

The British notes, answering the Soviet allegations, denied all knowledge of the activity of Commander Crabb near the destroyer, and expressed "regret at the incident."

There was no resolution of the mystery. Why had Crabb surfaced near the Russian ships? He must have known he would be observed. His colleagues in underwater work say he was having trouble with his oxygen equipment. Was he already dead at this time? One report states he was floating, face up.

The following year, on June 9, 1957, Royal Air Force men found a headless, handless body in frogman's equipment on a sandbar on Pilsea Island off Chichester Harbor in Sussex. Chichester Harbor is ten miles east of Portsmouth Harbor, where Crabb disappeared April 19, 1956.

Preliminary examination identified the rubber diving suit as "standard naval equipment." The local coroner, Mr. G. F. L. Bridgman, reported there was no evidence to indicate cause of death. On June 26, an inquest concluded by identifying the body as that of Commander Crabb. Identification was based on the diving suit, on body measurements, and on certain scars and minor skeletal malformations.

Commander Crabb was buried in Milton Cemetery, Portsmouth, on July 6, 1957. No official representatives of the Royal Navy were present.

Does this end the story of Commander Lionel Crabb?
"No," says journalist J. Bernard Hutton, who bases his answer on a "secret Russian dossier," major documents from which are shown in "Frogman Spy," Hutton's report on the disappearance. These records prove conclusively, Hutton insists, that Crabb did not drown in Portsmouth Harbor on the day of his disappearance, April 19, 1956. Instead, he was captured alive by the Russians, drugged and flown to Russia, brainwashed, and now works as an underwater expert in the Soviet Union, under the name First Lt Lev Lvovich Korablov.

The British Admiralty discounts this explanation of Crabb's vanishing. Through a high-ranking spokesman the Admiralty designates the book's story "a complete fabrication."

Whatever the final, true solution to the mystery, the record of Commander Crabb's vanishing has not strengthened the actuarial reasons for adding life insurance to the fringe benefits for espionage agents.

Further reading:

Brean, Herbert. The mystery of the frogman's dive for red secrets *Life* 40:38-42 May 28, 1956.
Hutton, J. Bernard. Frogman spy: The incredible case of Commander Crabb.
Pugh, Marshall. Frogman: Commander Crabb's story.

Amelia Earhart

THE AIRY HEART

When Amelia Earhart vanished in mid-Pacific on her
globe-girdling flight in 1937, she was the world's best-
known woman flyer. Miss Earhart, in private life Mrs.
George Palmer Putnam, ranks with the great names
of aviation, who a generation ago ushered in the Space
Age. Today, twenty years after her disappearance, there
is still discussion of just what happened when she and
navigator Fred Noonan failed to reach a planned landing on tiny Howland Island.

"Lady Lindy" is a symbol of gallantry, modesty, and
devotion to an ideal. "A.E., " as she is known to many,
wore her laurels lightly. The flight records she established and broke read like the exploits of a dozen
people, but the overwhelming public acclaim of her
"stunts" A.E. received with disarming nonchalance. "I
fly better than I wash dishes," she said. "I fly for the fun
of it."

Amelia is probably the only trans-Atlantic passenger
whose baggage has been a poem. When she finished
her solo hop over the ocean from Newfoundland to Ire-

land in the spring of 1932, her personal effect of a tooth-brush was supplemented by a telegram from Lady Astor offering the loan of a nightgown. Ever since July 2, 1937 when banner headlines announced that Earhart and her navigator Noonan were down in the Pacific there have been persistent theories explaining how the fliers were lost, never to be heard from again:

The plane, specially designed for buoyancy floated to an isolated reef. The flyers, safe in their inflatable life raft and with adequate provisions of food and water, reached an uninhabited atoll near Howland Island. The plane was shot down by the Japanese because it inadvertently flew over Saipan, the Truk Islands, or another of Japan's key naval bases in the Western Pacific. The flyers were captured and killed or imprisoned by the Japanese after they successfully completed their secret mission of photographing Japanese military installations in the Pacific. The aviators died instantly when their plane, "The Flying Laboratory," overshot its destination, ran out of gas, and submerged when it hit the waves.

How do the facts answer the mystery of the Earhart-Noonan last flight? Amelia Earhart born in Atchison, Kansas, in 1897 spent her early life in a number of cities in the mid-West, attending a variety of schools as her family moved to accommodate the demands of her father's work as a railroad attorney.

Before the Earharts moved to California, Amelia had worked as an aide for the Canadian Red Cross and taken courses in biological science at Columbia University. In Los Angeles, her interest in a medical career was forgotten when she first went up in an airplane with Frank Hawks, famous World War I flyer, known for barnstorming flight exhibitions and his non-stop transcontinental flight records. On her first air adventure, starting from the old Rogers Airport at the corner of Wilshire and Fairfax, A.E. found her life-long love—to fly. To finance the expense of flying lessons, she worked as a postal clerk, took courses at the University of Southern California to learn photographic dark room work, and sold unneeded luxuries such as a fur coat and jewelry.

Amelia soloed after 10 hours of instruction and won her pilot's license in a Kinner plane, with a three-cylinder motor. After one year of flying, her longest solo flight was the thrilling forty miles from Long Beach to Pasadena. On December 15, 1921, she received a well-earned Christmas present: An international pilot license — the seventeenth issued and the first granted a woman by the Federation Aeronautique.

After several years more flying, further study at Columbia University and attending summer school at Harvard University, A.E. lived in Boston teaching extension courses in English to factory workers in the area for Boston University and working as resident social worker at Denison House, a settlement on Tyler Street. In the spring of 1927, a telephone call came from New York. It was the call she always waited for. The voice asked if she would fly as a passenger over the Atlantic. No woman had yet made this ocean hop, and her personal qualifications and interest in flying made Amelia Earhart the logical person for this "first."

Amelia agreed to the exciting offer. The caller, George Palmer Putnam, publisher and publicist, and A. E. were married four years later in 1931. The flight got off after several false starts from Newfoundland and twenty-one hours later when the "Friendship" was set down on its pontoons at Bury Port, Wales, the Atlantic Ocean had been flown over for the eleventh time, and Amelia was the first woman to cross by air. Two experienced airmen who piloted the 500 h.p. "Friendship," Wilmer Stutz and

Louis Gordon, labeled A. E. their ideal passenger. Forwardlooking news stories pointed out that such multi-motored hops made commercial trans-oceanic flight seem practical.

Within a year, Amelia flying alone piloted her super-charged Pratt and Whitney Wasp from Harbor Grace, Newfoundland to Londonderry, Ireland. On this one flight May 20-21, 1932, she became the first woman to solo the Atlantic, the first person to fly the Atlantic twice, and set records for the fastest Atlantic air cross-ing, for the air speed record of flying 2,026.5 miles in thirteen and a half hours, and the distance record for women flyers. She landed in the first possible open space after sighting land because her altimeter had stopped working. Beside this she was nearly out of gas using most of the 420 gallons over the ocean, and the plane had a defective exhaust that might mean fire. After taxiing to a stop, she jumped out and ran to a stolid farmer plowing near where the plane stood. "Where am I," she called. The farmer called back a location not in the geographies, "In Gallagher's Pasture."

A.E. was received by the Prince of Wales, the French Legion of Honor made her a member, Congress awarded her the Congressional Distinguished Flying Cross, and the National Geographic Society gave her its special gold medal, awarded by President Herbert Hoover, and placed her name on its honor role along with such pio-neer explorers as Charles Augustus Lindbergh, Sir Er-nest Shackleton, Admiral Richard Byrd, and Captain Amundsen. Appreciative of the awards and public ac-claim, but overcome by the press of publicity greeting her flight, shy A. E. commented, "I'll be glad when the zoo part is over."

For the next five years, 1932-1937, Amelia Earhart Putnam's life was happy and full with the things she

liked best. The Putnam house in Rye, New York, a gra-
cious pink stucco, became a meeting place for explorers
and adventurers such as William Beebe, Commander
Byrd. To make such world travelers at home, the guest
rooms were decorated with realistic murals showing a
jungle swamp, a South Seas marine garden with exotic
fish, sea plants and coral. Amelia spaced her article writing with lecture engagements all over the country. She
talked on aviation and her flights to a full range of
groups — Service clubs, Daughters of the American Revolution, university audiences. She even told the Women's
Christian Temperance Union that medical evidence
showed intoxication at high altitudes prolonged a hang-
over. The problem of financing her flights A. E. met in
part by work at Purdue University, where she was a visiting faculty member and counselor. A research fund of
$50,000 established by anonymous donors as the Pur-
due Research Foundation allowed for experiments directed to furthering the science of flight, and in attract-
ing and training women for new careers in the field of
aviation. By additional grants from Foundation members, Amelia was able to purchase a twin-engine Lockheed Electra, "The Flying Laboratory," for tests and
flights. This silver plane with its two Wasp "H" engines
and retractable landing gear had a cruising speed of 180
miles an hour. It represented the most advanced design
in aviation with an 1100 horse power motor directed to
lifting its 15,000 pound full-load. "The Flying Laboratory's" cruising range was "in excess of 4,000 miles,"
with twelve fuel tanks holding 11,500 gallons of gal-
oline.

As the work of maintenance and checking her plane
was done at Burbank's Union Air Terminal, the Putnams
moved to North Hollywood, a few minutes drive from
the Terminal in San Fernando Valley.

On January 11, 1935, A. E. soloed in record time from
Hawaii to Oakland. Flying at 8,000 feet, she established
a 15 hour and 47 minute east-west record for the hop.
Several months later, she made another speed record
from Burbank to Mexico City and flew on, May 9, to
New York City. "One last flight" remained in her system.
Amelia said this world flight following the equator,
would finish her flying career. In March 1937 as her
plane speeded down an extended air-strip in Hawaii a
blown tire or a burnt out shock absorber on the landing
gear caused a near accident. Amelia and the rest of the
crew jumped out of "The Flying Laboratory" unharmed.

To change the get away luck on the world flight, A. E.
reversed the original route. The change of plan, circling
east to west, saw Amelia and navigator Noonan flying
out of Miami Municipal Airport at 5:56 on the morning
of June 1, 1937. Back came frequent encouraging word at
each of their stops in Puerto Rico, Brazil, Africa, India,
Australia, and, finally, Lae, New Guinea. The next flight
was the longest and most difficult, an ocean hop of 2556
miles from Lae to Howland Island. The Island, so small
that the pin prick on the map exaggerates its actual di-
mensions of 1-1/2 miles long by 1/2 mile wide, is a low
coral atoll standing only fifteen feet above the waves at
high tide. Howland had been selected two years before, in 1935, as a stopping place for transport services
on the Honolulu-Samoa flight.

The aerial navigation required to hit the small target
of Howland Island allowed for no error. Dead reckoning
estimates of position, based on speed and direction of
flight weren't fine enough here. The celestial shooting
for a "fix" of the "Flying Laboratory's" position was navigator Fred Noonan's specialty. He had flown so often as
Pan-American navigator and member of the China Clip-
per crew on the China-Manila run, that such position-

setting and direction-finding were a routine part of his Pacific crossings.

At ten o'clock Friday morning, July 2, A.E. and Noonan left Lae for Howland Island. The two chronometers for shooting the plane's position from the stars couldn't be set exactly because of radio interference, but they had one sure location finder: The radio bearings sent from ships and from shore stations.

The United States Navy cruiser Itasca stood by off Howland to guide the flight. Commander W. K. Thompson had weather and bearing signals broadcast on the hour and half hour, and the "Flying Laboratory," in turn, was to send its position at fifteen and forty-five minutes past the hour. The radio wave lengths used were the frequencies of 6210 and 3105 kilocycles on the code letters KHAQQ, assigned the plane by the Federal Communications Commission. The plane's communication system also included a two-way radio telephone, in common use in ocean navigation, but one of the first installed on aircraft. George Putnam waited for relayed news of the flight in the Coast Guard radio station at Fort Funston, near Oakland, California. He had talked with A. E. by radio telephone from Cheyenne to tell her, "I'll be sitting in Oakland waiting for you."

No news of the plane had been received by 1 A.M., July 2, Howland time. The Itasca, as scheduled, was sending notice by voice and code giving position and reporting excellent flying conditions — ceiling unlimited and sea smooth. An hour later, at 2:45 A.M., the Itasca picked up the voice message on the radio-telephone on wave length 3105, " . . . cloudy and overcast . . . head winds."

The Itasca broadcast "A" signals, indicating position, and requested the "Flying Laboratory" to communicate by key code. No answer was received. After another message from the plane at 3:45, "Itasca from Earhart," stating they would listen in at 3105 frequency at the assigned times, it was apparent that there was radio trouble on the plane. No position bearings had been sent to the Itasca, key code was not used, the standard marine frequency of 500 kilocycles was ignored, and the voice messages were garbled and incomplete.

A. E. sent four more messages in the next hour from 7:42 to 8:45. She said that their gas was running low, that they had about thirty minutes more aloft, and that they were flying at 1,000 feet and circling but could not locate the Itasca or Howland Island.

The final message said:

"We are in line of position 157-337 . . . will repeat the message on 6210 kilocycles . . . Wait . . . listening on 6210 kilocycles. We are running north and south . . ."

Fifteen minutes later, at 9:00 o'clock, Commander Thompson reported from the Itasca to San Francisco, "Earhart unreported at 0900. Believe down." Judging by the eighteen hours flying time from Lae, the signal strength of the messages, and the thirty minutes of gasolene reported, the "Flying Laboratory" was calculated to be 100 miles from Howland. Considering the further messages, it appeared that the plane had overshot its mark and was flying away from its landing. As a landing was possible on Baker Island, forty miles southeast of Howland, the search for the plane began in the waters north of Howland Island. The seaplane that Commander Thompson requested from Honolulu was forced back by a sudden storm, but warships and planes had been dispatched to aid in the search for the plane before Mr. Putnam's request for a search reached the Navy Department in Washington.

The battleship Colorado came from Pearl Harbor, the aircraft carrier Lexington, with sixty planes, cruised full speed from San Diego. A search, and still another search was made of 104,000 square miles of water. The ocean remained calm in that area. All reefs, islands, atolls were scouted. Chance of survival was set by experienced seamen as one in a million. Mr. Putnam pointed out that with the special arrangements for buoyancy, "The Flying Laboratory" should be able to float indefinitely. With the calm seas, the distress signals of Very lights, rockets and flares should be sighted.

From all over the Pacific area, amateur radio operators reported signals from the downed plane. On July 4 a message was received, from A.E. by an operator in Wyoming, the next day at Honolulu Coast Guard Station, and the next morning Amelia Earhart's voice was heard by a radio man in San Francisco.

From these messages, Mr. Putnam thought the plane had come down on land as the underwing radio batteries had not been put out of commission by a water landing. The Itasca and other search ships moved to positions given by the reported messages from the flyers. They found nothing.

On July 11, eight days after the plane went down, Mr. Putnam acknowledged the help of the United States Navy and the Coast Guard, and the immediate search was abandoned.

No officially reported SOS or bearings had been received from "The Flying Laboratory," on its flight from Lae. In fact, only seven direction bearings had been sent on the whole world trip of over 23,000 miles. Commander Thompson, and other navigators, learned too late that the 500 kilocycle radio equipment in the plane was discarded just before the take off in Miami. It was jettisoned to save weight and avoid the trouble of reeling in the trailing aerial by hand on landings. There was no way for the Itasca to receive and send bearings to the flyers. When Fred Noonan joined the flight in Miami, he had borrowed a bubble octant for aerial navigation, replacing the ship sextant, the only equipment that had been provided to take celestial bearings. Another important aerial navigation device—zinc aluminum powder bombs to estimate wind drift over the ocean—was found left behind in Miami.

There were so many rumors at the end of World War II that the flyers had met with foul play, that the United States Navy made an official announcement explaining that Amelia Earhart was not on a naval mission when she vanished; that she and Fred Noonan had not been shot down by the Japanese; that they had not been rescued from the Japanese, or found dead in a Japanese prison.

The most authentic explanation of the tragedy is that of Commander Thompson, on the scene aboard the cruiser Itasca. It is his opinion that the radio failed on the plane, and that the flyers missing their Howland Island target could maybe, with a fortunate landing, have floated for an hour. The radio messages reported after the plane went down were not received by stations near the scene, and were the messages of rescue planes and ships which were mistaken for those from the Earhart plane.

In A.E.'s letter left to be opened if she didn't complete her last flight, Mr. Putnam read, "Please know I am quite aware of the hazard . . . " "When I go," she had often said, "I'd like to go in my plane. Quickly." That is probably just the way it happened.

Further reading,

Earhart, Amelia. Last flight of Amelia Earhart.

Elliott, Lawrence. Mystery of Amelia Earhart's last flight. *Reader's Digest* 71:110-6 July 1957.

Pitman, Jack. Amelia Earhart's last flight. *Coronet* 39:122-5 February 1956.

Putnam, George Palmer. Soaring Wings, a biography of Amelia Earhart.

Alexander I

THE SPHINX OF THE NORTH

Assassination is an occupational disease of the Romanoffs, rulers of Russia for three hundred years. This ruler's hazard probably skipped Alexander I, the fourteenth Romanoff Czar, but a mystery surrounds his death that has not been solved, even today. According to this persistent story, Alexander did not die in December 1825, as officially reported, but left the heavy burden of his crown to live as a hermit in Siberia for forty peaceful years after his reported death. Alexander I, in the same family as Ivan the Terrible, Peter the Great, and grandson of Catherine the Great, may not be the most famous of the Romanoffs, but he is the most mysterious.

As Czar and Autocrat of All the Russias, he presided over a brilliant, extravagant, and autocratic court unmatched in nineteenth century Europe. The court glittered with elaborate entertainments, great balls lasting the night, illuminated festivities with fireworks, torchlight parties, and lighting of intricately playing fountains. At formal dinners, guests, escorted by twenty footmen, rivalled each other in conversation and in rich cos-

tumes, bright with jewels, medals, and ribbon decorations. Intrigue was its order. In this setting of oriental
splendor, the etiquette of the court was prescribed by
detailed protocol. When presented to the Czar, a visitor
was shown through a series of anterooms, and, as the
last set of doors was thrown open, he entered the room
where the Czar stood, stopped a specified distance from
the Emperor, and upon presentation by a Master of
Ceremonies, made three low bows and stood ready to
answer any greeting or remarks addressed to him.

The Orthodox religion of the court provided an appropriate Byzantine decoration. Its color formed part of
the social pattern. Emotional scenes participated in by
the entire congregation marked the *Te Deums* attended
by the Czar and court, where, on holy days members of
the royal family were seen to prostrate themselves before
church dignitaries — falling on their knees, in the manner
of the East, to touch their foreheads to the pavement.

The tide of revolution that swept the western world
for a hundred years, starting in the 1750's, barely af-
fected Russian society during the years of Alexander I's
reign, 1801-1825.

Young Alexander, succeeding to the throne upon the
assassination of his father, Czar Paul I, attempted sweeping liberal reforms during the early years of his reign.
Tradition was strong, and abuses many. Under the gaiety
of court life, the ferment of social unrest grew. The
machinery of government was inadequate — there was
not even any system of courts; and social burdens heavy
— serfs were still traded for hounds. In the last few years
of Alexander's rule, popular discontent showed itself in
the number of secret societies dedicated to reform and
to establishing a constitution. Revolts and embittered
feelings showed in all levels of society. Czar Alexander
responded to these problems by transferring most of his

administrative powers to reactionary Count Arakcheyev. There was a revival of censorship of press and books, control of university education by requiring that teachers follow courses prescribed by the government, and limitation of communication with ideas outside Russia by forbidding the import of foreign books and restricting travel abroad. During this period, Alexander mentioned with increasing frequency his wish to leave the responsibilities of his position. He had served his country for twenty-five years. Even the officers in his army retired after this length of time. These were the years when Alexander curbed the power of Napoleon, who called him "The Northern Sphinx," and "The Wily Byzantine." The Czar was present at Austerlitz in 1802, signed the Treaty of Tilsit, rode at the head of the victorious columns entering Paris in 1814, and in the following year, dominated the Congress of Vienna and established the Holy Alliance.

In the autumn of 1825, Alexander, and his wife, Elizabeth, planned to leave St. Petersberg for a rest, because of the continued ill health of the Czarina. She suffered from a lingering lung infection.

They prepared to go to Taganrog, about a thousand miles from St. Petersburg on the Sea of Azov in the Crimea. This choice of place for convalescence of the sick Czarina is part of the enigma out of which the legend of Czar Alexander's death grew. Why did the Czar and his wife go to this small frontier town? It was a difficult twenty days journey from the capital, the climate was cold and damp, there were no suitable accommodations. Alexander left St. Petersberg on September 13, several days ahead of Elizabeth, to journey at his own speed and insure that the white brick Governor's house where they planned to stay was ready. Fewer than a dozen attendants formed the party. After the Empress arrived in Taganrog her health seemed to improve. Alexander took a short journey through the surrounding country. He returned to Taganrog with a fever on November 17. This was his final illness. Four days later news of his sickness was sent to his mother and brothers in St. Petersberg.

The following day, after a fainting fit, Alexander's mind wandered. His condition had not improved the next day, varying from delirium to coma. Poisoning was briefly suspected.

At Alexander's request on the morning of November 27, Father Fedotov, a local priest came to hear the sick Czar's confession and to administer communion. Czarina Elizabeth never left the Czar's bedside.

Two weeks after his return to Taganrog, on the morning of December 1, 1825, at ten minutes until eleven o'clock, Alexander I was reported to have died. After an autopsy was conducted, the body, according to the dictates of Orthodox ritual, lay in state for several days in the local church. After a delay of several months, never fully explained, the body was returned to St. Petersberg for burial. When the body reached the capital, it did not lie in state in the Cathedral, as was the usual custom. It was viewed at a night ceremony attended only by members of the royal family. Popular demand to see Alexander I in death became so strong that public demonstrations in the Kremlin required the use of armed force.

Over three months after his reported death, Alexander was entombed in the Fortress of St. Peter and St. Paul, burial place of the rulers of Russia.

The suddenness of the Czar's death, the delay in his burial, and the secrecy of the closed coffin give rise to a vast number of rumors. Eleven years later, in 1836, a hermit appeared in the village of Tomsk, in far away

Siberia. While hermits lived throughout Russia at this time, and holy men, noted for their sanctity, were protected by wealthy landowners proud to contribute for the care of a private hermit, this hermit achieved unusual notoriety. Known as Feodor Kouzmitch, the Tomsk hermit, is reported to have been treated with marked deference by the royal family and members of the court who saw him. Then too, Feodor Kouzmitch corresponded with a number of titled Russians. On several occasions, a friend or protege of the hermit, visiting in St. Petersberg, was treated to exceptional hospitality, and even presented to the Czar. In physical appearance Kouzmitch is described by a contemporary writer as "tall, broad-shouldered, with stately carriage." He closely resembled Alexander I. The story is told that an old campaigner, who had spent his life in the Russian army and seen Alexander many times, at sight of the hermit, saluted, crying, "It is our beloved Czar."

Feodor Kouzmitch died on January 20, 1864, forty years after the reported death of Alexander I, who would have been eighty-six years old at the time.

The legend of Alexander's survival as the hermit joined the roll of stories of the survival of public figures after their reported death. Seventy years earlier there was the enigma of the lost Dauphin of France. This legend produced nearly fifty pretenders to the throne of France, and years after the date of his supposed disappearance upon being smuggled out of his prison, discussion of the case required a special journal to print arguments proving and disproving the survival on the "Question of Louis XVII." Some seventy years later, there was considerable discussion of the death, or disappearance, of Adolf Hitler.

Does what is known of Alexander's character and personality, of his last illness, and of the autopsy, death

certificate and burial support the story that Feodor
Kouzmitch was the Czar?

When Alexander I was crowned Czar in 1801, there
was speculation as to just what part he had played in the
assassination of his father, Paul I. Whether his was
an active role, of whether, by inaction, he permitted
the murder, with its terrible scene of violence, there is
evidence that he felt great guilt. At the announcement
that Czar Paul was dead, on the night of his assassination, Alexander is reported to have sworn he would never
wear the crown with blood on it.

His political ideals of reform, and the visions of international accord based on Christian principles were far
from realized. In his later years, he felt that the popular
revolts, the secret societies, and the threats of personal
violence expressed the ingratitude of the people he had
tried to help.

During his reign he mentioned with increasing frequency that he would like to give up the crown, and to
return to a quiet, meditative, religious life. He felt
"crushed by the terrible burden of the crown." He was
increasingly religious, and given much to solitary walks
and contemplation. In the spring of 1825, Alexander told
the Prince of Orange, his brother in law, that he planned
to abdicate and lead the life of a private person.

While a careful description reports his final illness,
that description was allegedly written to order, some
time after his death. Cause of death is variously given as
malaria, typhoid fever, "disease of the liver," fluid in
the brain. Four physicians who independently reviewed
the record of his illness and autopsy years after his
death, agreed on a diagnosis. They stated that the person described died of syphilis. This finding was not sup-
ported by the known facts.

Dr. James Wylie, Alexander's surgeon, reports the illness and death in detail. But this is the same Dr. Wylie who certified the death of the murdered Czar Paul I as due to apoplexy. A generation passed before the truth of Paul's assassination became known.

A Dr. Tarassov who wrote the autopsy report stated in his memoirs that he did not sign the death certificate. His signature appears on the document. This proves, for some, that the official record of death is a forgery.

There are other unanswered questions. Why was no priest called for final rites within the last five days of the Czar's illness? He was strongly devout and the titular defender of the Orthodox church. Why did Czarina Elizabeth not accompany the body or go to the funeral in St. Petersberg? Illness was given as one reason.

Why was the Czar's mother reported to exclaim upon viewing his body, "Yes, it is my son?"

Immediately after death, Alexander's appearance is reported to have changed so greatly that he was not recognizable. Although the weather was cold in December in Taganrog, the body deteriorated so rapidly that two physicians who had seen Alexander several times immediately before his illness did not recognize him, after his death.

Rumors of the time suggested that a body other than Alexander's lay in his coffin. One report named Maslov, the Czar's courier who died a fortnight before his monarch the person buried as Alexander.

Because of continuing gossip about Alexander's death, his nephew, Czar Alexander II, is supposed to have had the tomb opened in 1865, forty years after the uncle's reported death. The coffin was found empty and removed from the tomb. The next Czar, Alexander III is also reported to have ordered the tomb opened to verify the rumor that Alexander I did not lie in the coffin. According to a contemporary source, the tomb was empty.

Considering the available evidence, it appears true that Czar Alexander I was discouraged by the failure to achieve many of his political ideals, that he was troubled by deafness and other physical disabilities, that he did find solitude and religious meditation a respite from the problems of state he could no longer face. It is not improbable that Taganrog may have been chosen a vacation site because of its remoteness and location would provide a relatively easy escape from Russia, that Alexander's death was fraudulently attested, and that the coffin placed in his tomb contained the body of another, or was empty.

All this may be true, yet it appears extremely unlikely that the Czar survived in the hermit. For a number of years before Kouzmitch found protection for his saintly way of life, he is reported to have earned his living as a day laborer working in a mine, in a vodka distillery. That autocratic Alexander, who changed the destiny of Europe, could have accepted these menial employments is incredible.

Modern historians are generally agreed that the legend that Alexander I lived after his officially reported death as hermit Kouzmitch has been discredited. Facts may deny the legend, but legends die hard.

Recently when the Soviet government moved the graves of the Czars, buried in the Fortress of St. Peter and St. Paul, they tried to deny a report that the coffin of Alexander I contained only a few stones.

Further reading:

Bariatinsky, V. Mysterious hermit *Fortnightly Review* 99:988-1001 May 1913
Gribble, Francis H. Emperor and mystic: The life of Alexander I of Russia

Jarintzoff, N. Legend of Alexander I, and the hermit, Theodor Kouzmitch *Contemporary Review* 101:856-65 June 1912
Paleologue, Georges Maurice. The enigmatic Czar

Charley Ross

THE STOLEN CHILD

The only sounds on that elm-shaded street in the quiet Philadelphia suburb the afternoon of July 1, 1874 were the familiar hoofs and wheels of a horse and buggy as it leisurely drove down Washington Lane toward the city. This ordinary occurrence introduced the tragic and still unsolved mystery of the disappearance of Charley Ross, age four years. The first widely publicized kidnapping in America, it was not until over sixty years later, with the disappearance of Charles Augustus Lindbergh, Jr., that the nation, and the world, was again so shocked by the stealing of a child — the most inhuman of crimes.

Today Charley Ross would be eighty-six years old. His parents never gave up the hope that he was alive. This is his story.

Charley Ross, a pretty, fair child with hazel eyes and blonde, curly hair, and his brother, Walter, two years older, looked forward to Fourth of July. They were inseparable playmates, and lived with their parents and five other children — two brothers and three sisters —in

Germantown, seven miles from the center of Philadelphia.

Christian K. Ross, their father, owned a large retail
grocery on the corner of Third and Market Streets in
the city. The well-ordered Ross home, set back in a
lawn among pleasant trees and shrubs, was maintained
by two maids, a cook, and a coachman. It was early summer, and Mrs. Ross was in Atlantic City for a short vacation with one of her older daughters. She had promised on her return in early July to give Charley and
Walter their outing at the seashore.

On the afternoon of Saturday, June 27, 1874, Mr. Ross
noticed traces of chocolate on the faces and hands of
Charley and Walter. Upon his question, they told him
two friendly men talked with them, when they were
playing on the sidewalk near the house, and had given
them candy. "Snatch racket" was not a part of the English language at that time, and Mr. Ross dismissed the
incident, feeling rather pleased that someone was fond
of his children.

When the children's two friends drove by the Ross
house again on Wednesday afternoon, July 1, Charley
felt he knew them well enough to tell them that he
would like some fireworks. Each afternoon of the two
previous days, the men in the buggy the children had
first seen on Saturday, had talked with Charley and
Walter and given them candy. They told their friends
their names, what their father did, where they lived.
When the men agreed to buy them fireworks, they willingly climbed into the buggy to drive for their treat.
As the buggy kept rolling through the streets, Charley
asked why they didn't stop and the men said they were
taking them to "Aunt Susie's" where they could buy a
whole pocketful of fireworks for a nickel.

When they reached Palmer and Richmond Streets in

downtown Philadelphia, eight miles from the Ross home, the men gave Walter a quarter, and he ran to the store pointed out to buy firecrackers and sparklers. A few minutes later when he came to get in to the buggy, he couldn't find it. The men and Charley had vanished, and he was lost.

A passerby, Mr. Valentine, attracted by the crying child, found out his name and where he lived. At eight o'clock that evening, just as Mr. Ross and a friend were leaving for the police station to report the boys missing, Mr. Valentine brought Walter home.

Walter's story increased Mr. Ross' alarm. When he asked where Charley was, Walter told him, "Why he's all right. He's in the wagon."

Mr. Ross and his friend went on to the police station and when they told the circumstances of Charley's disappearance, the police assured them that this was probably a drunken prank and that Charley would be found within the next few hours.

Mr. Ross then went to the area where Walter had been found, Kensington, a northern district of Philadelphia. There was no trace of Charley. Mary Kidder, the Ross' next-door neighbor, had told Mr. Ross she saw the children with two men in a buggy. Several other people remembered seeing the two children as the buggy drove toward Philadelphia. No one could be found who had seen Charley alone with the two men. The falling-top buggy, with its red-striped wheels and blue lining, and the dark bay horse could not be traced, then or at any later time.

Two days later no word of Charley had been received. On this day, July 3, Mr. Ross had put an advertisement in the *Public Ledger:*

"LOST. On the first instant, a small boy about four years of age, light complexion, and light curly hair.

A suitable reward will be paid for his return to
E. L. Joyce, Central Station, corner of Fifth and
Chestnut Streets."

While Mr. Ross was extremely worried about Charley,
up to this time neither he nor his friends thought his
son's disappearance other than a case of a child lost in
the city. It had not occurred to them that the two men
had deliberately taken the boy to hold him for ransom.
A second advertisement on July 4 offered $300 reward
for the return of Charley, who was described in more
detail:

"long curly flaxen hair, hazel eyes, light skin, and
round face, dressed in a brown linen suit, with short
skirt, broad-brimmed straw hat, and laced shoes.
Lost between four and five o'clock."

Shortly after July 1, 1874, Mr. Ross and the Philadelphia police saw that this description of Charlie Ross
was sent on thousands of broadsides to law enforcement
agencies in the United States and in other countries,
and to newspapers throughout the world.

* * *

CHARLIE BREWSTER ROSS, ABDUCTED
FROM GERMANTOWN, PENNSYLVANIA,
JULY 1, 1874
DESCRIPTION: Four years old May 4th, 1874,
body and limbs straight and well formed, round,
full face, small chin, with noticeable dimple; very
regular, and pretty dimpled hands; small, well-
formed neck; full, broad forehead; bright, dark
brown eyes with considerable fullness over them;
clear, white skin; healthy complexion; light flaxen
hair of silky texture, easily curled in ringlets, when
it extends to the neck hair darker at the roots,
slight cowlick on left side where parted; very light

eye-brows. He had no blemish, mark or scar, on any part of his person, except from vaccination on one arm. He talks plainly, but is retiring, and has a habit of putting his arm up to his eyes when approached by strangers. His skin now may be stained and hair dyed, or he may be dressed as a girl, with hair parted in the center.

*　*　*　*　*

The following day, the fourth day after Charley's disappearance, Mr. Ross received the first of twenty-three letters sent by the kidnappers. Postmarked July 4, Philadelphia, the letter was addressed to "Mr. Ros."

It said that Charley was safe and well, cautioned Mr. Ross not to go to the police, warned him that he would never find Charley, and ended by saying he would hear from them in the next few days. Great care had been taken to make the writer, who signed himself "John," appear illiterate. The handwriting was a disguised scrawl, common words misspelled, no punctuation used.

The police considered this the letter of a harmless crank.

Two days later on July 7, when Mr. Ross received a second letter, they decided that the writers were holding Charley, and that his life was probably in danger. This letter demanded $20,000 ransom. It told Mr. Ross that if he did not pay the amount he would murder his own child, and would be shown the corpse. There were terrible threats and warnings not to go to the police. As a signal of acceptance of the kidnappers' terms for the return of Charley, Mr. Ross was to publish an advertisement in the *Public Ledger:*

"Ros, we be willing to negotiate."

The police took action that was widely publicized.

They guarded all roads out of the city, searching wagons, buggies and trains. They started a house-to-house search for Charley. A reward of $20,000 was posted, by subscription, for "evidence leading to the capture and conviction of the abductors of Charley Ross, and the safe return of the child."

Time dragged on, with the police advising Mr. Ross, and the kidnappers being vague about how the demanded ransom would be paid. After a dozen or more letters from the kidnappers, a letter was received postmarked "New York City."

The kidnappers had told Mr. Ross that all their letters would be addressed "Ros," or "Mr. Ros." Each letter contained description and information about Charley so as to leave no doubt that he was in custody of the writer. The letters said Charley was anxious to get home in order not to miss his vacation in Atlantic City, and gave other unmistakable details showing that the child was their prisoner.

This first letter from New York told Mr. Ross to get $20,000 in small bills, put them in a bag painted white, and take a ticket on a certain evening train out of New York. He was to be on the observation car and when he saw a light or a white flag waving, in the dark along the track, he was to throw the bag toward the signal, and not stop until he reached the next station. Charley would then be returned in a few hours.

Mr. Ross complied with the directions, but instead of the money he put a letter in the bag. This letter demanded to see Charley alive, and agreed to the simultaneous exchange of the boy and the money. No signals were observed. A news article had reported that Mr. Ross had gone to trace Charley in another area, and the next letter from the kidnappers referred to the information in the article and told Mr. Ross he had made a mistake in not following the train directions.

A month after the disappearance, Chief Walling of the New York City Police Department, acting on a tip, had the extortion letters examined. Chief Walling said that the writer was known to the New York City police, and identified him as William Mosher, alias Johnson. His informant, Mosher's estranged brother, told how Mosher and his partner, John Douglas, alias Clark, had tried to get him to join them in kidnapping one of the Vanderbilt children earlier that year, in April. Mosher was a fugitive, having escaped from jail where he was being held for robbery. He and Douglas were itinerant peddlers of an insecticide, "Mothee," that they manufactured. They had their own horse and buggy. Philadelphia was their headquarters at the time Charley Ross disappeared. Mosher and his wife and children shared a house there with Douglas.

Mr. Ross, now answering the kidnapper's letters in the *New York Herald*, had given up temporizing and consulting with law enforcement agencies. When a letter was received in the middle of November ordering him to be at the Fifth Avenue Hotel to give the $20,000 ransom to a messenger, who would know nothing of the contents of the package given him, Ross agreed. As instructed, he put an advertisement in the *Herald*, "Saul of Tarsus, Fifth Avenue Hotel," and gave the date, November 18, when the money would be delivered. All day on Wednesday the eighteenth Ross' two representatives waited with the ransom money. No messenger appeared. That was the last letter received.

Mr. Ross hired Pinkerton detectives to investigate the case. There was a stream of children reported as Charley Ross from all over the country. Several more weeks went by as Mr. Ross and his agents continued checking all clues.

On the night of December 14, over five months after the disappearance, two burglers were shot when they attempted to escape from the summer home of Presiding Justice Charles Van Brunt of the New York State Supreme Court. Judge Van Brunt's brother, living next door in the fashionable Bay Ridge section of Brooklyn, surprised the robbers as they were leaving the vacant house. When the men fired on Van Brunt, and on his son and two employees, they were shot. One man, William Mosher, died instantly. The other, John Douglas, badly wounded, said he had something to tell them.

As he lay dying in the light of lanterns, sheltered from the heavy rain by an umbrella, Douglas confessed, "Mosher and I stole Charley Ross." He said that he didn't know where Charley was hidden, but that Mosher would tell them. To convince Douglas that his partner was dead, Mosher's body was shown to him.

Douglas then said that Charley would be returned safely in a few days. He continued, "He is . . . ," became unconscious and died in a short time. Charley was not delivered to his home. He was not brought to any public place, although Mr. Ross had designated a number of places where $5,000 would be paid for the return of Charley, with no questions asked.

Mrs. Mosher, and her brother, a man named William Westervelt and a former policeman in New York City, were questioned by Chief Walling. Westervelt was questioned many times, offered his police job back, and offered immunity in the kidnapping for information about Charley. All the information he or Mrs. Mosher would give was that they believed Charley to be alive. Mosher had agreed, several days before his death in the robbery, that holding Charley was too risky, and he was going to send him home. Mosher's wife said that her husband would never have been capable of harming

Charley. Westervelt was convicted and sentenced to seven years imprisonment in solitary confinement at hard labor as an aid and an accessory in the abduction.

In February, 1875, the year following the kidnapping, the Pennsylvania legislature passed a law making twenty-five years imprisonment the penalty for abducting or detaining a child. To encourage the return of Charley, who was believed still alive, a special provision was included in the law. Any person delivering a stolen child to the nearest law enforcement agency on or before the 25th day of March 1875, would, by the law, be immune from any punishment.

No person appeared with the missing child.

Mr. Ross continued his search for his son. He or his agents talked with nearly three hundred children reported to be Charley. Sixty thousand dollars was spent in his twenty-year investigation. The disappearance of Charley Ross became a classic American mystery, and although the boy's name, picture and description were known to millions of people, there was never any direct news of him after that Wednesday afternoon of July 1, 1874, when he rode with the two men in their buggy. When her husband died twenty-three years after the kidnapping, Mrs. Ross continued looking for Charley, still hoping he would be found alive.

Many claimants came forward through the years asking for a share of the Ross wealth, but none was acknowledged to be Charles Ross. As late as 1939, Gustave Blair, a sixty-nine year old carpenter, established his identity as Charley Ross to the satisfaction of a jury of merchants and cattlemen in the superior court in Phoenix, Arizona. Although the jurors decided Blair's claim was valid and the Arizona court permitted him to assume the name, "Charley Ross," the other Ross children, defendants in Blair's bid for recognition as a mem-

ber of the Ross family, refused to recognize him as their
missing brother. Charley Ross may have died shortly after he disappeared in 1874. He may still be living.

The day that the Ross family, and a sympathetic
world, looked forward to never arrived. They were never
able to say, "The lost is found. Charley Ross is home
again."

Further reading:

Macarthey, Clarence E. Charley Ross, the unforgettable
lost boy *Ladies Home Journal* 41:7 July 1924
Ross, Christian K. The father's story of Charley Ross
Smith, Edward H. The Charlie Ross enigma, pages
1 - 22, *in* Mysteries of the missing

Richard Halliburton

THE DEATH OF THE *SEA DRAGON*

The report that Richard Halliburton, American author and lecturer, was missing at sea late in March 1939 was at first thought to be another of his press-agent stunts. Sailing from Hong Kong in a Chinese junk, the *Sea Dragon*, with a crew of fourteen, his destination was Treasure Island, site of the World's Fair in San Francisco. There, in its prearranged mooring, the colorful oriental sailing ship was expected to be one of the most popular concessions. An equally important goal of the voyage was the lecture, article and book material such high adventure would provide Halliburton.

Riding a post-war wave of demand for romantic and glamorous exploration, Dick Halliburton became the alter ego of millions of arm-chair travellers. His syndicated articles appeared in fifty newspapers with a combined circulation of over nine million, the first two accounts of his travels were on the best seller list at the same time, and his shy personal manner and boyish good looks had endeared him to thousands of lecture audiences, not all of whom were women's club members. When such a

celebrity dropped from sight on an exciting and publicized venture, immediate speculation as to his fate
produced a tangle of rumors. Reports implied that the
ship's vanishing was just another box-office appeal angle
to insure interest when it arrived at Treasure Island; that
the ship had been captured as a rich prize by pirates
thronging the waters out of Hong Kong; the *Sea Dragon*,
with a bright red hull, became the easy target for a
Japanese warship; the junk was too frail to ride out the
devil's weather of a tropical typhoon, and was wrecked
with all hands.

Only several weeks before on a shake-down cruise of
the *Sea Dragon*, Halliburton had identified himself as
the world's worst sailor, and, although barely out of the
sight of land, all he prayed for was anything to end the
terrible "oscillation." What had happened to cause his
ship to vanish with no trace when it had gone only a
third of its way on the 9,000 mile voyage?

Soon after Richard was born on January 9, 1900 in
Brownsville, Texas, the Halliburton's moved to Memphis,
Tennessee. There Wesley Halliburton, Richard's father,
made a comfortable living as a real estate broker, and his
mother, Nelle Nance Halliburton, enjoyed an active life
of clubwork, and incidental teaching of practical psy-
chology to school and other groups.

Richard early demonstrated his wanderlust. When he
was seventeen, his mother saw him off on the train for a
weekend visit with a cousin in a nearby town. Four days
later, when the family heard from Dick, he was in New
Orleans shipping out as a sailor for Europe. This first
adventure on the sea, and the excitement and strangeness
of Paris, where he lived for a year, set his life course.
Never again long in one place, he tried to live always at
the crest of the wave. He could barely wait to graduate
from Princeton to wander off on his Royal Road. Even

while he attended college, the pull of adventure proved too strong. Wearied with routine class-attending, he spent his junior year touring Europe. The next year a forward-looking dean let him continue with his class. After editing the *Princeton Pictorial* in his senior year, Dick Halliburton graduated from Princeton in 1921.

Four years later, *The Royal Road to Romance,* his first adventure book became a best seller. Halliburton liked to recall that the manuscript, rejected by nine publishers, was accepted by the tenth only because the editor reading it had heard him tell of his adventures at a Princeton Club meeting.

His second book of travel fables, *The Glorious Adventure,* followed the first in popularity. By the Halliburton formula, the newsworthy events of history lived again in a you-are-there motif. With superb showmanship, he followed the wanderings of Ulysses from Ithaca and back, scaled Mount Olympus, swam the Hellespont with Leander, climbed over the Acropolis walls by moonlight, rode an elephant with Hannibal over the Alps, and heard the death-bed confession of an assassin of Czar Nicholas II of Russia and his family. In South America, he followed the conquistadores route of Cortes in Mexico, dived into the sacred well of the Mayans at Chichen Itza, retraced Balboa's march across Darien to the Pacific, swam by installments through the Panama Canal. In Asia, he climbed snowy Fuji Yama in mid-winter, swam at night among the lily pads in the forbidden pool before the Taj Mahal, hiked through mystic Tibet. He trudged, jumped, scaled, swam and flew through seven books of personal adventure that sold over a million copies annually years after they were first published.

With him, his readers and lecture audiences, swam in the Sea of Galilee, spent the summer on Devil's Island, marched—for a day or two—with the French Foreign

Legion, reached the peak of the Matterhorn, looked into the crater of Etna, rested on the slopes of Popocatapetl, explored the Marathon race course, visited the oracle at Delphi, were held up by Chinese pirates, and sat penniless in Monte Carlo.

Before he was thirty, this slight, careful adventurer was famous and rich. Explaining he was too roving for marriage, Halliburton maintained a bachelor pent house in New York, and a home overlooking the Pacific at Laguna Beach, California. When his first two books went into twenty editions, he thought that luck, but, he confessed in an autobiographical statement, when they were translated into "a couple of dozen foreign languages, I felt convinced they must be unusual books."

Some of his critics found the premeditated casualness and thorough exploitation of his adventures annoying, and condemned his frantic commercialism. Others spoke of his bad writing and superficial reporting.

In the middle of his thirty-eighth year, the summer of 1938, Halliburton conceived the idea of sailing a Chinese junk 9,000 miles across the Pacific from Hong Kong to the San Francisco World's Fair. Early in the planning of the exploit, the Chinese merchants offering financial backing for the voyage dropped their assistance because they feared Japanese warships would interfere with the junk's sailing. While the immediate project of spectacularly arriving in the Golden Gate, appealed to Halliburton, he was just as interested in undertaking the sail because it would prove a "colorful and dramatic" opening for his next book: *Royal Road to Romance in the United States*. His story of the voyage of the junk would become the first chapter in the relived epic of American history, representing a "pre-Columbian discovery of America." With a budget set at $25,000 for the sailing, Halliburton raised more than that amount in several months. Dissuading voices concerned with the safety of the mid-winter crossing of the ocean in a ship not designed for such a voyage, he answered just as effectively. He told Horace Epes, manager of Consolidated News Features, subsidiary of North American Newspaper Alliance, distributor of his newspaper accounts for publication, that even if a storm carried away the main mast and disabled the auxiliary engines, the ship would make sixty or seventy miles a day.

His father's doubts, Richard disregarded, urging him not to worry and assuring him that everything was properly safeguarded. The captain and the key men of the crew were experienced seamen, the hull would be divided into water-tight compartments, and even the lifeboat had a sail. Upon his arrival in Hong Kong, a tour of the waterfront with his skipper, Captain John Wenlock Welch, and Engineer Henry von Fehren showed that it had been easier to find a name for their junk, the *Sea Dragon*, than to find the actual boat. A seaworthy junk was three times what they could pay. The only solution was to build an ocean-going junk to specification. Within days construction on the best of all possible Ningpo-type junks was under way. While Welch and von Fehren worried about keels, thickness of hulls, rudders and other seamanlike problems, Halliburton arranged the decoration and supervised other less concrete features of the junk.

He saw to the traditional beating of gongs and lighting of fire works, the Chinese way of driving away the demons of storm and shipwreck. He supervised the installation of the great black eyes on each side of the prow. Following an ancient custom, to open the eyes and make them good to see through any weather, a priest beat drums, attached paper prayers, bathed the eyes in rice wine, and set off firecrackers. These were the usual measures followed in launching a Chinese junk, and all of them were necessary to placate Tai Toa Fat, the god of sailors and fishermen.

On final sailing day, March 4, 1939, the local press agreed that no more beautiful junk ever put out from Hong Kong harbor. The *Sea Dragon*, a striking sight with hull painted brilliant Chinese red, striped white and gold at the rail, showed twenty-foot red and yellow dragons on each side. The Chinese good luck symbol, a multi-colored phoenix, appeared on the stern. The three-masters sails of orange, scarlet and white complemented the large gold Chinese characters, "*Sea Dragon*, Hong Kong," above the luck charm. Built with extra sturdy timbers, the seventy-five foot junk carried two tons of food — three months provisions for the crew of fourteen, and 2,000 gallons of water. Fuel for the auxiliary engines filled the remaining storage room. There was enough for ten or twelve days.

A week out of port on March 13, the *Sea Dragon* radioed, "1200 miles at sea. All's well."

Six days later another message, "Halfway Midway arriving there April 5 . . . " was received in San Francisco.

Four days more of sailing and the third message came from the *Sea Dragon*. Riding seas forty feet high, the liner *President Coolidge*, largest passenger ship in service on the Pacific, was proceeding through a typhoon at six knots an hour. The *Sea Dragon*, nineteen days out of Hong Kong on this night of March 23, was still 1200 miles west of Midway Island. Dale Collins, executive officer of the *President Coolidge*, received a radio message from his friend Captain Welch, master of the junk, *Sea Dragon*:

"Southerly gales, squalls, lee rail under water . . .

wet bunks ... hard tack ... bully beef ... having wonderful time ... wish you were here instead of me.

Welch, Master"

After this last message, the *Sea Dragon* and all members of its crew vanished. The United States navy Cruiser *Astoria* searched an area of 150,000 square miles of sea. They found no trace of the junk or survivors. Dale Collins, in a report published in the *United States Naval Institute Proceedings* of June 1939, concluded

"If the *Sea Dragon* encountered such weather as we did on the night of March 23, and she undoubtedly did, there is small chance that the little craft survived."

In early October of 1939, a chancery court jury in Memphis, Tennessee declared Richard Halliburton legally dead on March 23 or 24—the only uncertainty that he perished in a tropical typhoon and the time of his death due to the nearness of the *Sea Dragon* to the international date line on the night of its last message.

It was eighteen years since Dick Halliburton reported his first adventure of scaling the Matterhorn. The cruise of the *Sea Dragon*, undertaken with the same drive and excitement of his youth, was Halliburton's last glorious adventure.

Further reading,

Halliburton, Richard. The famous adventures of Richard Halliburton.

Roger Charles Tichborne

Arthur Orton

THE MISSING HEIR

"FOUNDERED WITH ALL HANDS."
On this brief announcement posted in Lloyd's of London
to report the fate of the *Bella*, three-masted schooner out
of Rio de Janeiro for her home port, New York, rests a
Victorian mystery that entertained England for over a
quarter of a century. Appropriately, that chapter of the
story starts in 1854 with a drunk-sodden figure smuggled aboard the *Bella* under cover of darkness, as she
road at her moorings off the Gamboa wharves. This lone
passenger, Roger Charles Doughty Tichborne by name
and scion of one of England's oldest families, was heir to
a title with extensive lands and a fortune paying an annual income of nearly one million dollars. The *Bella*
sailed April 2, 1854 from Rio.

The ship, her master, William Birkett, forty members
of her crew, and her passenger Roger Tichborne never
reached any port. On the basis of this fact, and the reported findings of a capsized longboat marked "Bella"
floating near a ship's wreckage some four hundred miles
off the Brazilian coast, the schooner was presumed lost.

A London court declared Roger Tichborne legally dead the following year in July.

While the court ruled Roger perished in a shipwreck, his mother never gave up the hope that he might have been rescued. With a singleness of purpose her relatives testified amounted to monomania, she continued to advertise for her lost son as a "missing person" in newspapers and journals of the day. Twelve years after the supposed wreck of the *Bella* her faith was rewarded by news from Australia that her son Roger still lived.

This began the strange history of "The Claimant," the Tichborne imposter, whose controversial identity stirred the public imagination for years. From the evidence brought out in mountains of testimony; over 10,000 printed pages — in the civil trial of The Claimant in his attempt to prove he was the heir Roger Tichborne, and from the subsequent criminal trial of The Claimant for perjury, the courts reached definite legal conclusions about the identity of the purported heir. However, the public, including members of Parliament and of the Bar, did not all accept these judicial findings.

By court decision The Claimant was declared to be Arthur Orton, "an illiterate butcher." His bold deception and its near success was considered by many a sad commentary on human gullibility. Perhaps an equal number of persons distributed throughout the educational and social levels of society thought the pretender a man cheated of his inheritance by legal trickery. If The Claimant was not Roger Tichborne, did Roger survive the shipwreck of the *Bella?* Was he found drifting with several crew members in a lifeboat and carried to Australia on the schooner *Osprey?* Did he willingly join in the plan of the *Bella's* captain and crew to steal the ship by changing her appearance and name and to sail her to the Australian gold rush? One observer close to the

Techborne case appraised it by saying, "It is incredible that The Claimant was Roger Tichborne; it is even more incredible that he was not."

What really happened to Roger Tichborne, England's most famous missing heir? Roger Charles Doughty Tichborne was born in Paris on January 5, 1829, of a French mother and an English father. His beautiful and charming mother, Henriette Felicite, was the natural daughter of Englishman Henry Seymour and possessed a considerable fortune in her own name. She completely dominated her husband, James Tichborne. James was the third son in the Tichborne family. As his chances of inheriting the family title and money were remote and did not demand residence in England, and as his wife much preferred to live in France, Roger spent the first fourteen years of his life in Paris.

Mme. Tichborne's "Dear Roger" grew up a slender, cultured French boy. Stories of his childhood report that he was dressed in skirts to the age of twelve, and that this mother was jealous of the tutors who provided his early education. When deaths in the Tichborne family made it clear that Roger would someday be the eleventh baronet and master of extensive England lands, James Tichborne took his son to Stonyhurst, the famous "Catholic Eton" for further training. Mme. Tichborne sent a family servant to bring Roger home from England, and upon his refusal to return, she was so hurt that she did not write to him for over a year. Roger pursued the usual studies of the day, including Latin, Greek, mathematics, but as he was an indifferent scholar, he left Stonyhurst in 1849 to find a career in the army.

After some preparation he passed entrance tests in fortifications and other military subjects and joined the Sixth Dragoon Guards. As a subaltern, stationed in Dublin, Roger began his service in The Queen's Army. Roger

was a soldier in direct opposite to the bluff, sturdy "By
Gad, Sir" British officer. The tailor fitted him for his uniform only with great difficulty, installing special hooks
to hold up his trousers because his twenty-three inch
waist and small hips furnished no anchorage. Tichborne's differences in manner, interests and appearance
from his fellow officers did not go unmarked. Roger became the butt of innumerable practical jokes and con-
tinuous hazing. Several times women were hired to wait
for him in his bed, and once a mule rested in his sitting
room. As he was a good sport about these boyish capers,
Roger was generally well-liked by his army companions,
but after three years soldiering, Roger sold out his commission planning to engage in the more compatible occupation of travel and residence abroad.

During his time in the army, he had fallen in love
with his cousin, Katherine Doughty. Kate, the daughter
of Roger's uncle Edward, lived at Tichborne Park in
Hampshire. In correct Victorian manner, Roger had
never mentioned his affection to his cousin, but he did
discuss it in detail with his aunt, Lady Tichborne. She
saw certain objections to the match — in many letters
she chided Roger for his excesses in smoking, drinking
and reading French novels, but at the same time, she
was not indifferent to her nephew's future inheritance.
Finally she agreed that after a wait of three years, if her
daughter had not found a more suitable husband, they
might marry.

It was to fill this interim of waiting that Roger,
twenty-four years of age and with a comfortable allowance, decided on a world tour. On March 1, 1853, he
sailed from Le Havre on the *La Pauline* for Valparaiso,
Chile. He found South America romantic and rich in
the exotic birds and flowers of his current interest. He
toured Chile and Peru, crossed the Andes to Brazil, sent

home a collection of brilliant bird skins from an expedition's shooting with native guides.

From Rio Roger wrote to his mother telling her he was leaving South America and would probably go to Australia. Roger was now immediate heir to the Tichborne title and fortune as his father succeeded to the baronetcy five days after his son sailed on his world tour. With an allowance increased by 1,000 pounds a year, Roger planned only to continue his travels. He wrote to Gosford, the steward at Tichborne Park, "I am sorry my mother's character is so disagreeable, because it must make Tichborne a kind of hell for my father and everybody in the house." Roger also instructed Gosford to be prepared to provide living quarters for Lady Tichborne far from Tichborne Park when he would succeed to the title. To his mother, he wrote complaining that even in her letters she treated him as though he were twelve or thirteen years old, and told her that she would not hear directly from him again.

The *Bella*, a new schooner carrying a cargo of coffee along with some ballast to fill her run, scheduled a voyage to New York by way of Kingston, leaving Rio April 20, 1854. This was the ship Roger Tichborne sailed on as a traveller that never returned. According to the later testimony of Captain Oates, who identified himself as a good friend of Roger, he agreed to pay the boy's passage, because Roger was temporarily out of funds, but as the young Englishman had been drinking a good deal, had no passport and no time to get one before sailing, he smuggled Roger aboard early on the morning of April 20. The ship sailed on schedule for Kingston, her passenger having been hidden when the Brazilian officials checked the schooner just before she cast anchor. The *Bella* was never seen again. Four days later on April 24, a ship off the coast of Brazil reported seeing a lifeboat

with her name and some floating wreckage. The own-
ers of the *Bella* listed her as lost with all hands. There
was some speculation as to how a new ship proved seaworthy in several voyages could have struck a leak. One
theory of the wreck was that the ship's goods were care-
lessly stowed so as to make her topheavy. She capsized
in a storm that did not bother better managed schoon-
ers.

Although Roger had been declared legally dead, and
his younger brother, Alfred Joseph, succeeded to the
Tichborne fortune in 1862, Dowager Lady Tichborne
never doubted that he was alive and well. There were
rumours the same year that the *Bella* vanished, and several years later, that survivors of the wreck had been
picked up from a lifeboat and taken to Australia.

When, after twelve years, Roger was reported living near the southeast coast of Australia in Wagga-
Wagga, New South Wales, Lady Tichborne was prepared to receive him as her son.

The arrival of The Claimant in England a year later,
thirteen years after Roger Tichborne's death had been
accepted, and the trials beginning in 1871 to prove that
he was not the missing heir but an audacious imposter,
are reported in newspapers, cartoon books, pamphlets,
"alphabets," and court records.

The Claimant's physical appearance so differed from
Roger's that one witness sarcastically observed, "A race
horse has been turned into a cart horse." While the
height of the two men was approximately the same
(5' 8 or 9"), their stature and weight differed greatly.
Roger had weighed 160 pounds; the man from Australia
tipped 26 stone (364 pounds). Other less immediately
observable physical differences were brought out in the
trials as scars, tattoos (Roger had RCT below a cross,
anchor and heart — for "Faith, Hope and Charity"—

on his right forearm), and formation of particular facial features (Roger's earlobes were attached, The Claimant's free). Dowager Lady Tichborne complained that Australia had caused a coarsening of her aristocratic son, and although his statements differed from hers, she accepted him as the missing heir. She died before the trial to prove The Claimant's identity. Hundreds of other witnesses gave testimony that The Claimant was in truth Sir Roger. Family servants, Tichborne Park neighbors, Roger's school friends at Stonyhurst, and his fellow army officers swore the Australian was Roger returned from the dead. All other members of the Tichborne family, and many others testifying in court, denied that The Claimant could be Roger.

In his first letters to his mother after reappearing in Australia, he did not even know her Christian names. He did not recognize his father's handwriting, members of his family, and other intimates of his life in Paris, England and Ireland. He could no longer speak French, his native language; he was not able to recognize a text in Latin and one in Greek, though he had studied both at Stonyhurst.

Perhaps the greatest difference was in his character, manners, attitudes. The Claimant's profession of deep sentiment for his "Dear Mama," was opposite to Roger's acid appraisal of his mother's character. Also, The Claimant said he had seduced his cousin Kate Doughty, and that she tried to get him to marry her because she was pregnant. This statement was proved false by all other evidence.

Forensic elocution, in its height as public entertainment in Victorian England, used these dramatic materials for a long-drawn courtroom battle. Social leaders, the diplomatic corps, publicly prominent men and women all clamored for special admittance and seats to the

trials. Some were shown special courtesy by being seat-
ed with the judges hearing the spectacle. Evidence
of the seduction of Kate Doughty, of a secret malforma-
tion of Roger and The Claimant were more outspoken
than plays or books of the era. In establishing Roger's
character, excerpts from the French novels he had always been reading were declaimed by counsel. Because
of their risque nature, the women in the court room
were asked to leave while the novels were being read
into the record.

The question of The Claimant's identity took on social and political coloring, and there was feeling that the
legal proceedings were a vindication of the Common
Man against the entrenched Privileged Class. Authorities prepared to meet threatened riots for "Good Old
Roger," several times during and immediately after the
trials.

The hundreds of witnesses called gave contradictory
testimony on each detail. The ship rescuing passenger
and crew from the wrecked *Bella* was identified as the
Osprey, in accordance with The Claimant's story. Other
testimony denied existence of such a ship as the *Osprey*.
Testimony was given to show an Englishman identifiable
as Roger Tichborne was known in Australia, that a ring
he sold was identified by a jeweler in the Australian port
where he landed from the *Osprey*, that both he and
Arthur Orton had been seen together in the Australian back country. This testimony was balanced by
evidence showing the *Bella* a total loss. Her captain and
none of her forty crew members were ever found to testify.

The Claimant's attempt to prove that he was the miss-
ing Roger Tichborne was "non-suited," the case dropped.
In the "Tichborne Estates Act," passed in July 1874,
Parliament declared Roger Tichborne dead and author-

ized the trustees of the Tichborne estate to pay the great costs of the court battle to protect the family's interests: 90,000 pounds.

The Crown's criminal case against the pretender on the grounds of perjury, proved that the imposter was Arthur Orton, the adventurous twelfth child of a poor London family. He was sentenced to fourteen years in prison for perjury on several counts. Released after serving a ten year term, Arthur Orton found he had dropped from the public interest. He never gave up his claim of being Sir Roger, and when he died April 1, 1898, thirty-three years after coming to England as the missing heir, his coffin bore the metal plate:

Sir Roger Charles Doughty Tichborne.

The Tichborne family had allowed this final grace, but no marker indicates the burial place in a London cemetery.

Not explained is Orton's testimony showing a knowledge of intimate details of Roger Tichborne's life that could not be gained from any amount of reading available public accounts of his disappearance, thoroughly studying his letters and family records, or by talking with his friends, acquaintances and associates.

Several solutions have been offered to explain The Claimant's knowledge -- He must have been well-acquainted with Roger when they both lived in Australia during the years 1854 to 1863, and so acquired a mass of details about Roger's early life to know exact conversations, insignificant happenings, personal mannerisms of his friends and family. Another explanation, one mentioned even by a member of the court hearing the evidence, was that The Claimant was an unrecognized illegitimate child of some member of the Tichborne family, and through close association with one or more of the family had acquired a knowledge of events and associates. No proof ever made these theories fact.

The trial of The Claimant, England's most famous impostor, legally proved his impersonation fraudulent. It left unanswered the question of whether Roger Tichborne was lost at sea in a shipwreck of the *Bella*.

Futher reading:

MacGregor, Geddes. The Tichborne imposter.
Woodruff, Douglas. The Tichborne claimant.

Percy Fawcett

THE SECRET OF THE MATO GROSSO

Jungle sounds deep in the interior of Brazil sang a siren song for Colonel Percy Harrison Fawcett, this century's most celebrated lost explorer, and lured him to an unknown fate. "The forest in these solitudes," he wrote, "is always full of voices, soft whisperings . . ." It was these voices that called him back time and again to the uncharted forests of the Mato Grosso and neighboring states, and on his eighth and last journey in 1925, he disappeared into the wilderness with two companions and no authentic trace of his party has ever been found.

Colonel Fawcett may well be the last famous explorer of this earth, considering the current interest in astronauts, moon colonies, and space travel. In the thirty-five years since he vanished little more has become know of the region he entered. Now airstrips make the journey to Brazil's interior easier by shortening the tedious days of canoe and land travel, and some additional information results from the work of individual scientists and the S.P.I. (Servico de Proteccao aos Indios), Brazil's enlightened Indian agency, but that area of Brazil's "Great Woods," between the Xingu and the Aragaya Rivers, still represents the largest unexplored spot on this planet. The fastnesses of Africa, and the frozen acres of the poles have been probed to record scientific information about their geography, weather, plants, animals, and human inhabitants. For the "Fawcett area" no two maps agree, and information reported routinely for other regions of the earth is shown for large sections of the Brazilian jungle as "Unknown," "Doubtful," or marked "?."

The story of Colonel Percy Fawcett, former officer in the English army, a trained engineer whose first experience in South American exploration was as the surveyor in the delimitation of the boundary between Bolivia and neighboring countries in 1906, continues an intriguing mystery, primarily because of the purpose of his last expedition.

Financed and equipped by England's Royal Geographical Society, of which he was a Founder's Medalist, and by the North American Newspaper Alliance, he planned to record observations for mapping of the area he traversed, and to send back dispatches or stories, as he was able, for newspaper articles. His personal objective was far removed from these sober activities. The expedition was really a search for "Z," his designation of a fabulous lost city, older and more wonderful then the ruins of Egypt, rich in treasure and still inhabited by clothed white people, the civilized remnant of its ancient builders. For many years Colonel Fawcett had been interested in stories of buried treasure and lost cities. As a subaltern in the Royal Artillery stationed in Ceylon, shortly after 1900, he searched for the buried treasure of the Kandyan Kings. For eighteen years in South America and England, he pursued the legends of lost mines, buried cit-

ies, abandoned treasure. He believed wholeheartedly
in the existence of "Z," as described in the log of
a Portuguese expedition of 1743. This record (Manuscript no. 512, Biblioteca Nacional do Brasil) described a monumental lost city high on an unscalable
cliff on the Central Plateau of Brazil. Its only ap-
proach up a steep crevice made passable by paving
and some steps, the entrance to the city was marked
by three tall arches, which lead to great courts and
ceremonial buildings. Extensive inscriptions showed
in the weathered stones.

Only ten years before, Hiram Bingham on an expedition for the National Geographic Society and Yale
University had reported the findings from the great city
of Machu Picchu in the Andes. This and other archi-
tectural monuments in South America, such as Cuzco,
the former capital of the Inca empire, and the imposing
fortress Sacsahuaman showed a long line of local civilizations pre-dating the Incas found by the Spanish and
Portuguese conquerors. They too had been described in
detail in old documents of the sixteenth and seventeenth
centuries.

Discovery of "Z" should provide answers in fact to
archaeological questions concerning origin of forgotten civilizations and knowledge of pre-Columbian
settlement of South America.

Inquiry as to the fate of the Fawcett party began
about two years after they were last heard from. Since
1927 the quest for information regarding the lost explorers has never stopped. Great numbers of individuals
and groups entered the jungles of Brazil with the main
or incidental purpose of finding Colonel Fawcett. Rescue parties searched for the rescue parties. Ill equipped
and casual parties were so numerous that the Brazilian
government restricted entry to those sections of the

Indian country to searchers with certain jungle travel experience and preparation.

"Official" rescue teams, such as that led by Commander George Dyott, searches by Brian Fawcett, the Colonel's younger son, and hundreds of other expeditions reported their findings in statements, articles, books, and papers. Through the years repeated solutions to the mystery of the lost explorers proved ill-founded or purposely misleading. Colonel Fawcett was seen as a rancher in the Brazilian interior. He was held captive as a white God by a primitive tribe in the rain forest. He was murdered by Indians of the Chavante, the Kalapalo, the Suya, the Aruma tribe. He found "Z," the lost city of his search, and was making careful observations of the great community and of the life of "Z-men." He was stranded in the jungle without adequate equipment or strength to return to civilization.

What facts can be sifted from the mass of jungle gossip, rumour, and legend surrounding the fate of the Fawcett party?

Colonel Fawcett, skilled in land navigation in the jungles, belonged to the "old school" of explorers. He acted as an individual, avoiding group explorations, and refusing to be one of a party on expeditions composed of experts — geographers, botanists, zoologists, and anthropologists. His geographical and archaeological explorations since his release from the British army in 1914 had centered in the little-known region of central Brazil ranging from the headwaters of the Tapajos River on the west to those of the Tocantins River on the East. This area, a vast flood plain for the Amazon and the Araguaya Rivers, included the tributary streams of the Xingu River and the Araguya River, such as the Rio das Mortes or River of Death.

Previous significant exploration of the region was lim-

ited to that of the Bandeiros, the "flag" troops of three
hundred or more armed Portuguese who penetrated to
the interior of Brazil to develop the mineral wealth, the
journeys of Karl von den Steinen, famous German eth-
nologist, who descended sections of the Xingu River in
1884 and 1887 from Cuyaba, Colonel Roosevelt's expedition down the River of Doubt in 1914, and the
explorations of the rubber workers.

When he entered the jungle on his last journey, his
only companions were his elder son, Jack, and his son's
friend, eighteen-year old Rodney Rimmel, son of an English naval surgeon. Because of the physical barriers in
the area to be explored — rough land, flooding rivers,
thick forests with many trees one hundred feet tall,
primitive Indians noted for their treachery and cruelty, myriads of insects, snakes and other wild animals,
the Fawcett party travelled light. They carried enough
food to last for about three weeks and planned to live
off the jungle. On their planned route, pack animals were
not practical because of scarcity of pasture and the numbers of blood-eating bats. The tropical forest tribes they
would meet and need to make friends with for provisions and guides were divided into tight, self-con-
tained tribal units. Each tribe fearful of and warring
with its neighbors had acquired civilization from the
Whites, whom they may have met years ago, so that
instead of killing their enemies for trophies or to eat
them, the Indians had learned to capture their neighbors to sell them into slavery.

Colonel Fawcett and Jack arrived in New York City
from London in mid-December, 1924. After meeting the
third member of their party, Rodney Rimmel, who
joined them from California, and completing business
arrangements for the expedition, they sailed for Rio
de Janeiro on January 11, 1925. The route they pro-

posed to follow, as stated in the plan submitted to the Royal Geographical Society, and reported in the Colonel's books and articles showed an estimated two years journey:

> Leave civilization at Cuyaba, capital of Mato Grosso state, Brazil.
> Proceed north with mules to Paranatinga River.
> Canoe down Paranatinga to about 10° south latitude.
> Strike across country, roughly northeast, to the Xingu River, proceeding on foot through the forest, following the watershed.
> Further cross country to the Araguaya River.
> Cross the Tocantins River.
> On across the Sao Francisco River near Chique-Chique.
> Visit deserted city described by explorers of 1743 (approximately 11°30' south latitude and 42°30'10" west longitude).
> Strike railroad at Bahia City, returning by rail to Salvador on the east coast.

Following this plan, Colonel Fawcett, Jack and Rodney Rimmel started into the Mato Grosso from Cuyaba at the beginning of the dry season, early in April 1925. They knew that the flat flood plain, the drainage basin for the Amazon, north of Cuyaba would be passable only in the several dry months of the year. Two Mufuquas Indians accompanied them to help with the pack animals on the first leg of the journey.

A month later on May 7, the Colonel wrote to the Royal Geographical Society in London that he expected to reach unexplored high country after about two months' travel. The next, and last, letter the Society received August 4. Sent from Bakairi military post, dated May 20, the Colonel warned that he was "about to go out of communication."

Nine days later Mrs. Fawcett received her last letter from her husband headed "Dead Horse Camp," where he had previously camped in 1921. The next word, dated May 30, the North American Newspaper Alliance, sponsoring the expedition, received in Rio de Janeiro in November. This dispatch was the last authentic word from the Fawcett party. It was sent back by the two Indian mule tenders, who proved reluctant to continue into the unknown dangerous country and so returned to Cuyaba from Dead Horse Camp.

From the Camp's position, 11°43' south latitude, 54° 35' west longitude, about midway between the Paranatinga and the Xingu Rivers, it appeared that the Colonel had changed his announced plan of canoeing down the Paranatinga. Instead, he struck out northeast overland. This change in route bears out the report of friends and relatives of the Colonel who believed his announced route only a "smoke screen" for his real journey. Extremely secretive about his information on the Lost City, "Z," he had stated many times that an explorer couldn't "potter about the rivers," which in the area near Cuyaba were relatively well-travelled and well-known. He had also remarked that "Z" wasn't to be located on the Xingu River or anywhere in the Mato Grosso.

As the party expected to be gone at least two years, travelling in country where it would be impossible to send back letters or dispatches, it was not until October 1927 that inquiries were sent by the British ambassador in Rio to the Brazil foreign office requesting information concerning the fate of the Fawcett expedition. On the basis of investigations of Indian agents in the interior, the Governor of Mato Grosso state reported that before reaching 11° latitude the three explorers had branched east in the direction of the Araguaya River. There was no further news of the Fawcett party. It was believed that the explorers had been killed by one of the tribes living along the Xingu river.

A farmer at Paranatinga stated that one of the dogs taken with the expedition returned to his farm in an emaciated condition sixty days after the party left for the Xingu.

Roger de Conteville (Courteville), a French civil engineer, reported seeing a sick white man on the road in Minas Gerais. He thought that the elderly white-bearded man must be the missing Colonel Fawcett. Other travellers in the area stated that Colonel Fawcett was a "gentleman farmer" in the unexplored interior. The Colonel was reported seen east, north, west, south of Cuyaba.

Commander George Dyott, financed by the North American Newspaper Alliance, entered the *sertao*, unexplored back country, in May 1928 from Cuyaba with a fully equipped "Fawcett Relief Expedition," of twenty-six men, including cameramen, radio operators, and three tons of equipment. His mission to find news of the Fawcett party, he reported the long-waited for news: The three explorers were killed by Anaqua (Anahukua) Indians in July 1925, or perhaps they had been murdered by Suya Indians.

The Fawcett family, and many others, did not accept these findings as closing the Fawcett story.

Two years later in 1930, Albert de Winton, a journalist, led an expedition to find traces of the missing explorers. He returned to talk again with the Kalapalo concerning the fate of Colonel Fawcett. He never reappeared. The Kalapalo tell one story that they feared he had come to avenge the murder of the Colonel, so they murdered him, buried him under leaves until his bones were bleached, then threw his skeleton into a lake.

Vincenzo Petrullo's findings are similar to those of Commander Dyott. Petrullo, on a field trip for the University Museum in 1933, was told by Indians that the Kalapalo ferried the Fawcett party over the Kuluene River, and saw the smoke from their camp for six nights as they walked through the high grass of the *Plan Alto,* the plateau between rivers. The Indians found the last camp of the explorers one hundred miles west of the Rio das Mortes. No further trace of them was found.

A year later, the Churchward expedition exploring the Rio das Mortes was told a similar story. The Kalapalo's chief said he found traces of a massacre at the last known camp, eleven marches from the Kuluene River. The Aruma Indians must have killed the party.

Missionaries of the Inland South America Missionary Union were given a similar account by the Indians. The explorers' food had run out, but the Colonel insisted they continue on their journey. Out of mercy and because they knew the explorers would starve, the Kalapalos murdered them about five marches east of the Kuluene River. This account agrees in general with that given Dyott and Petrullo.

At various places in the jungle articles identified as belonging to Colonel Fawcett were found — a metal tag, a uniform case, part of a theodolite. None of these was considered conclusive proof of his death, or even that he had passed in the area. Several articles were reported to be those discarded on previous expeditions.

In April 1951, Orlando Vilas Boas of the Central Brazil Foundation reported a "final chapter" of the Fawcett mystery. Several days journey in Kalapalo territory, he

had been shown the grave of Colonel Fawcett, murdered
by the Indians for threats and insults — he slapped a
chief in the face. The skeleton sent with care to London for examination was announced by the Royal An-
thropological Institute as definitely not that of the
Colonel. Their examination was based upon teeth and
known stature. In fact, their report continued, the bones
were probably not those of a white man.

As Colonel Fawcett was nearly sixty years old when
he disappeared in the jungle, there is little chance
that he still lives. His son Jack and Rodney Rimmel,
forty years younger than the Colonel, might still be
alive in the remote Brazilian back country.

Brian Fawcett, the Colonel's younger son, checked
the bearings of the Lost City "Z." He found no trace of
a city, or of the explorers. Several years ago he proposed to buzz each village over a range of some 40,000
miles of jungle, dropping questionnaires with instruc-
tions for hand signals to find out whether the two
younger explorers lived among an unknown Indian tribe.
Mrs. Fawcett always maintained that her husband and
son, Jack, were alive and would someday return. For
some years, the Britch government agreed with her as
during this period she never received the army pension
that would be paid to her upon verification of the
Colonel's death.

Recent explorations in the Mato Grosso touch only
the edges of the heavily forested, little explored regions,
reported rich in unexploited mineral resources, and a
"Lost World" of isolated plant and animal life.

The population of known Indian tribes in the area
has shrunk to a tenth of the number reported twenty-five
years ago. Trained anthropologists who have lived
briefly with some of the more accessible tribes have tried
to dispel certain fictions about these primitive people

— that they are like children, that they will kill a white man on sight. Trained observation of these Indians does show clearly that the stories they tell white men with whom they are friendly, are often the reports that they think their visitors would like to hear. They possess little sense of time, number and distance as known by the white man. In one instance, Indians told a traveller that a certain camp was "less than fifteen minutes away," and it was reached after a two days' journey. Legend and history often merge as one.

From the available information, it appears that the Fawcett party probably died within several months from May 30, 1925, the date of the last dispatches from Dead Horse Camp. Whether they died of thirst, hunger, exposure, sickness, or were killed by Indians is not known. The full story cannot be told. From time to time each year, the motors of Beechcraft and Piper Cubs disturb the solitude of the Mato Grosso forests. Most of the of the time there is only the voice of the jungle. It has never revealed the fate of the Fawcett party.

Further reading:

Burton, Richard Francis. Exploration of the highland's of Brazil. Appendix: English translation of the report of the 1743 discovery of the Lost City (Manuscript no. 512, Biblioteca Nacional do Brasil)
Churchward, Robert. Explorer lost; the story of Colonel Fawcett
Colonel Fawcett's expedition to the Matto Grosso *Geographical Journal* 71:76-85 February 1928
Dyott, George Miller. Man hunting in the jungle; being the story of the search for three explorers lost in the Brazilian wilds

Fate of Colonel Fawcett *Geographical Journal* 88:66-72
   July 1936
Fawcett, Brian. Ruins in the sky
Fawcett, Percy Harrison. Lost city of my quest *Black-
   wood's Magazine* 233:88-97 January 1933
Fawcett, Percy Harrison. Lost trails, lost cities
Fleming, Peter. Brazilian adventure
Weyer, Edward. Jungle quest

Jesus de Galindez

Gerald Murphy

THE ABSENT PhD

Of the 8,903 PhD degrees conferred by colleges and universities in the United States for the academic year ending in 1956, 203 were granted in the field of political science. One of these 203 degrees in the study of government, Columbia University awarded to Jesus Maria de Galindez on June 6, 1956, *in absentia*. Why the good doctor was not able to appear in person to claim this educational honor, wearing the traditional uniform of cap and gown, is a question with a simple answer. He had disappeared.

His disappearance, one of the two most mysterious vanishings of modern times, is usually considered with its twin enigmatic absence and discussed as the "Galindez-Murphy Case."

Among the incidents that must be fitted together to explain the Galindez truancy are: A $35,000 blood-money payoff; the midnight flight of a chartered plane carrying a swathed unconscious figure; a forged suicide note; picketing the White House; a band of hired killers called "The 42;" masked figures on a nation-wide newscast; a half a million dollar whitewash job; and characters called "The Dead One," and "The Limping Man."

How does this space-age melodrama play?

The main character is Jesus de Galindez, a forty-two year old Spanish Basque lawyer and journalist, and a Roman Catholic anti-Communist, a graduate-student instructor at Columbia University. For six years he also acted as the agent of the Basque-Government-in-Exile. Because of outspoken criticism of political dictatorships, specifically that of Rafael Trujillo in the Dominican Republic, he was fearful of violent reprisals. On Monday March 12, 1956, after dismissing his evening class in Hispanic-American Civilization, that met from 7:40 to 9:20, at Hamilton Hall, he accepted a ride to Columbus Circle from one of his students, Evelyne Lang. The professor hurried through the swirling snow, briefcase in hand, toward the subway entrance at 57th Street and Seventh Avenue. It was 9:45 P. M. That was the last time he was seen. His friends were quick to point out that he was the victim of a political plot after the pattern of murder-for-hire engineered by Trujillo. It was reported that his body had been crammed whole or piecemeal into the boilers of the *Fundacion*, a Dominican ship in New York harbor at that time. He had absconded with half a million dollars he short-changed the organization he represented. He was murdered and robbed by an unknown thug. He had secretly flown to Spain to organize the underground against Franco. He was acting as a Soviet agent in Budapest. He had joined his Communist friends in Russia. He had been abducted and flown out of the country to the Dominican Republic, where he was "disposed of" on Trujillo's orders. It was this last theory that introduced the second principal character: Gerald Lester Murphy.

A 23-year old pilot whose home town was Eugene, Oregon, "Gerry" Murphy flew a chartered plane that left a Long Island airport shortly after midnight of March 12, 1956, the day Galindez vanished. His only passenger on the flight was a "wealthy invalid" carried aboard the plane from an ambulance.

After refueling in Florida, the plane landed at Monte Cristi airport north of Ciudad Trujillo, the capital of the Dominican Republic. With this flight, Murphy's luck changed. He was able to purchase for $3,412 cash a new Dodge convertible, where days before he was broke. In several weeks he moved to Ciudad Trujillo where he flew as co-pilot for the Dominican airline, *Compania Dominicana de Aviacion*. He lived well — bought another car and maintained an apartment in both Miami and Ciudad Trujillo, knew some of the important people in the city, and became engaged to a Pan-American airline stewardess. Murphy's preparations to return to the United States were nearly completed on December 3, almost nine months after the Galindez' disappearance, when he too vanished.

His car, found abandoned off the road on a high cliff by the sea, offered no clues. Gerald Murphy has never been found. The United States diplomatic representatives in the Dominican Republic requested a full search and report for this missing American citizen. When Ambassador William Pfeiffer found a fellow worker of Murphy's who seemed unduly resentful of the boy's reported boasting the fact that he had been given his flying assignment on the direct orders of Trujillo, he reported these facts to the Dominican authorities. Although this fellow pilot, Octavio de la Maza, denied any knowledge of Murphy's disappearance, he was detained in the Ciudad Trujillo jail. Within several days, he was reported to have hanged himself in his cell, leaving a suicide note confessing that he had accidentally killed Murphy and was hanging himself out of remorse. What evidence links Murphy and Galindez? Is there any proof of the bizarre charges involving abduction and multiple murder?

Five days after Jesus Galindez disappeared on the snowy night of March 12, 1956, his friends reported him as a missing person to authorities. Since that night he had not been seen, failed to answer his telephone, and to appear for appointments. Police believed he reached his 30 Fifth Avenue address — the evening newspapers were in the apartment, and a dark gray overcoat found over a chair was identified as the one Galindez wore when he left Columbia University for his home. They could not determine whether he spent the night there. The apartment was not disturbed, but his abductors may have been waiting.

Among the mass of papers—there were eighty file drawers of scholarly, business, and personal information—a letter, dated October 4, 1952, informed the finders that if anything "happened" to Galindez the men causing his death or disappearance could be found in the pay of Rafael Trujillo, the Dominican dictator.

Jesus de Galindez, born in Madrid, attended the University of Madrid, receiving a law degree. After fighting with the Loyalists in Spain's civil war, and participating in the short-lived Basque Republic, as a member of the losing side, the Basque Nationalist Party (Catholic Democrats), he went as a refugee to France when Franco's Falangist forces crushed the last resistance in Spain.

In 1939 he was among a number of political refugees from Spain who were welcomed to the Dominican Republic, in an effort to increase trained and professional immigration.

Galindez' legal capabilities and pleasant manner found him various employments during the six years he lived in the Dominican Republic. He was a teacher; he acted as legal advisor to the national Department of Labor; and he became Secretary of the Dominican Minimum Wage Committee. In this last post, toward the end of 1946, he made a finding favorable to striking workers in the sugar industry. Upon this decision, contrary to government interest, he was dismissed from his public employment.

At this time, he moved to the United States and soon established himself in New York City. Galindez supplemented a modest income as Instructor at Columbia University by giving legal advice on complicated problems of international law, by journalistic and other writing, and by acting as fund-raiser for the Basque-Government-in-Exile. During the seven years he was a registered representative for the Basque group, he reported, in semi-annual statements filed with the United States State Department, over a million dollars received from his solicitations and campaigns for the Basque exiles, some $30,000 being listed for personal expenses.

Scheduled to receive a Doctor of Philosophy degree from Columbia University in international law in June 1956, Galindez had worked for a number of his years in New York in preparing a dissertation that would be acceptable for this graduate study. Titled, *The Era of Trujillo*, his 750-page documented thesis details the workings of a dictatorship in a South American setting.

There has been no trace of Galindez since the night of March 12. No hat, umbrella, eye-glasses guided the search for the missing scholar. In the thirteen-state police alarm and the careful investigation at the time of his disappearance, and later when the Murphy mystery was linked with his vanishing, there was no indication that personal or financial problems caused him to voluntarily absent himself or commit suicide.

The assertion that his body had been burned in the boilers of the Dominican ship, *Fundacion,* was proved false when it was shown that the apertures to the boilers were dollar-sized openings.

The reports that he had gone to Russia, was seen working as a Soviet agent in Budapest, left to work in the underground against Franco in Spain were unverified.

The charge that Galindez ran away or was "sequestered" because his accounts for the Basque organization showed a shortage of half a million dollars was denied by the President of the Basque group, Jose de Aquirre, from his headquarters in Paris. "Every cent was accounted for," Aquirre stated, showing records that the Paris office received $500,000, and $500,000 was sent to the Basques in Spain and to other Basque groups all over the world.

All these solutions had been suggested as answers to Galindez' disappearance by the Dominican government. They branded as "ridiculous libels" any implication of Trujillo in Galindez' death or disappearance. In Washington, a United States Justice Department spokesman reported the results of a detailed invetigation, "We have no facts to indicate Galindez was alive after March 12, 1956."

From previous investigations in New York City, it did appear that the Dominican government had been involved in several telemurders of New York City residents.

On April 28, 1935, Sergio Bencosme was shot to death in his New York apartment, 87 Hamilton Place, apparently mistaken for his friend Dr. Angel Morales, who had been exiled from the Dominican Republic since the elections of 1930 when he ran against Trujillo and lost. Bencosme lived long enough to identify Luis ("Chichi") de la Fuente Rubirosa, a Dominican consular official, as one of the gunmen. Rubirosa was indicted by the New York Grand Jury, but before he could be questioned he returned to the Dominican Republic. Investigators were then told he had met with a fatal accident.

The second reported political liquidation was the murder of Andres Resquena, editor of an anti-Trujillo Spanish-language newspaper on October 2, 1952. Resquena was shot six times in the dim-lighted hall of a lower Manhattan apartment lobby, and the running figure in the dark alley was never identified.

Before Galindez disappeared, he had been threatened repeatedly by agents of the Dominican Republic by letters and anonymous telephone calls. He feared for his life and had reinforced the locks on the door of his apartment, took precautions to keep his address "confidential," and had reported his apprehensions to the New York City police and to the F.B.I.

It was nine months after Galindez disappeared, when Gerald Lester Murphy vanished in Ciudad Trujillo, that the searches disclosed evidence that the two mysteries might be aspects of the same enigma.

Murphy, brought up on a South Dakota farm, had lived with his parents in Eugene, Oregon, worked as a draftsman, and flown for an air taxi company in Miami, Florida. His poor eyesight, even corrected by thick-lensed glasses or contact lenses, kept him out of the Air Force or from commercial flying, but he had earned a commercial pilot's license.

A time schedule of Gerald Murphy's activities immediately before and after March 12, 1956, the day Galindez disappeared, shows the following activities:

March 5   Murphy at New Jersey's Linden Airport chartered a twin-engined Beechcraft D-18 plane (N68100) to fly a group of businessmen to Miami. Cash rent receipt for $800 made out to "John Kane." Murphy's friend, Air Force Servicemen Harold French introduced to Arturo Espaillat (Dominican consul in New York City), one of the two men with Murphy.

March 6-10 Murphy discussed a mysterious flight with French, showed him maps, saying, "I will be taking somebody from Miami to Dominican Republic."

March 10-11   Extra gas tanks installed, increasing range of plane to 1500 miles, for trip to "Azores."

March 12   Murphy flew out of Newark airport 9:44 A.M. with announced destination Miami, Florida. Landed 10:30 A.M. Zahn's Airport, Amityville, Long Island. Waited through the day and until after midnight, when an ambulance arrived. Anthony Frevelle, night watchman, told his daughter and several others that the passenger carried from the ambulance to the plane "could not move a muscle." Frevele died in September 1956 of a coronary thrombosis before he was called to give his testimony.

March 13   Murphy landing at Tamiami Airport, Miami, was told gas pumps weren't open so early. Flew on to Lantana Airport, West Palm Beach filling tanks with $95 gasoline. A telephone call from New York City several days previously arranged for early morning refueling. Donald Jackson, mechanic,

who filled gas tanks in passenger compartment of
plane, reported seeing a body on a stretcher and
spoke of a "peculiar stench" he thought was a drug.
Jackson, subpoenaed to tell his story, died in an air-
crash six days before he was to testify.

Murphy left Lantana 8:00 A.M. Reportedly landed
at Monte Cristi Airport, north coast of Dominican
Republic. Landed at Tamiami Airport 4:30 or 5:00
P.M.

Next month, in April, Murphy began flying as co-
pilot for the Dominican airline. November 17, 1956,
after seven months in the Dominican Republic, he
wrote his parents that "his stay had served its purpose,"
and he was returning to the United States. His engage-
ment to Celia ("Sally") Caire, pretty airline hostess,
probably influenced this decision, as they were to be
married in less than two months, on January 10.

December 3 Murphy advertised his household goods
for sale in *El Caribe,* Ciudad Trujillo newspaper. That
same day he spent several hours with Sally, who was in
town for that brief time between flights. He told his fian-
cee that he had been summoned to a five o'clock appointment that evening at the presidential palace. He had
confided to Sally, and to others, that the "cancer pa-
tient" he flew to the Dominican Republic in March was
Galindez.

Three days later, the American embassy in Ciudad
Trujillo learned that Murphy was missing. Police said
that they found his abandoned car near the edge of an
ocean cliff on the morning of December 4 and assumed
it was stolen. When Murphy did not answer requests to
claim his automobile, they investigated and found out
he had not been seen since December 3. The United

States diplomatic representatives, William T. Pfeiffer, the Ambassador to the Dominican Republic, and Richard H. Stephens, charge d'affaires, urged official investigation and report on Murphy's fate.

According to the official report received March 16. 1957, Murphy's fellow pilot, Octavio de la Maza, had confessed the accidental killing of Murphy in a suicide note he wrote in the Dominican jail before he hanged himself. They had scuffled on the edge of the cliff where Murphy's car was found after he made improper suggestions and insulting remarks to de la Maza. Murphy fell over the cliff. The ocean below was filled with large sharks attracted to that area by wastes discarded from an adjacent slaughterhouse. No trace of Murphy was found.

After Stephens, charge d'affaires, tested the shower arm from which de la Maza supposedy hung himself, and after the F.B.I. examined the suicide note (certified as authentic by a Spanish handwriting expert, Professor Manuel Ferrandis Torres of the University of Madrid), the United States State Department rejected the Dominican Report of the solution of Murphy's disappearance and death.

They stated that the suicide note was a forgery, that Murphy's income, was far in excess of his $350 a month, plus overtime pilot's pay, and his friendship and association with highly-placed officials in the Dominican government were unexplained. Also they had definite evidence linking Murphy with Galindez' disappearance from logs, notes and letters in Murphy's writing, and other testimony.

About this time, Murphy's parents received a $35,000 draft on a Dominican Bank, supposedly a civil court judgment against the de la Maza estate for his part in the death of their son. As the money left by de la Maza could have been nowhere near this award, it has been assumed that the payment was made by, or at the request of, Trujillo. Mr. and Mrs. Murphy did not accept this payment. They consider contributing it to further the search for their son.

Over a period of months after the disappearances the *New York Times* reported the findings of Grand Jury and other investigations. Dominican representatives labelled the paper the dupe of Communists. *Life* magazine in its February 25, 1957 issue gave details of the vanishings in a lead article, "The story of a dark international conspiracy." The case was given further airing by CBS, in an hour documentary, "The Galindez-Murphy Case: A chronicle of terror," broadcast on May 20, 1957. Although fifty witnesses could not be persuaded to testify because they feared reprisals if their voices were recognized, others agreed to the appearance with the provision that they be masked to avoid identification.

Charles O. Porter, Congressional Representative from the fourth district in Eugene, Oregon, where the Murphy family lives, follows a tireless pursuit of the facts of the pilot's disappearance. He has made a trip to South America, checks reports of the status of the investigation from the State Department and the Justice Department, and urges a Congressional investigation of the disappearance and sanctions against the Dominican Republic.

To answer the public protest against the unsavory facts and circumstantial evidence linking Trujillo to the Galindez-Murphy disappearances, Sidney S. Baron, top-flight New York City public relations agent was retained. by the Dominican government. Baron engaged Morris Ernst, well-known liberal attorney, and special advisor on government projects for President Roosevelt and President Truman, to prepare a report of the case. Ernst accepted the assignment, commenting, "The Galindez case is a great mystery; I hope to solve it."

His "Report and opinion in the matter of Galindez," released after a ten month check, under the supervision of Ernst and former New York State Supreme Court Justice William H. Munson, surprised no one by finding "not a scintilla of evidence" linking the missing Murphy with Galindez' disappearance. Trujillo had refused to let Arturo Espaillat, deeply involved in the Basque's vanishing, testify in the United States at an official inquiry of the case. Ernst's unofficial inquiry in no way took the place of the official investigations, and it could not be considered an objective finding when subsidized by Trujillo, suspected of complicity. The report, designated the "$500,000 Whitewash," cost $562,855 to prepare. This figure was disclosed at a Grand Jury investigation. Also indicted by the same investigation was John Kane, the Dominican Republic's agent, with Murphy, when he rented the Beechcraft he flew from Florida. A Federal District Court jury convicted Kane, under his true name of John Joseph Frank, of failing to register as a representative of Trujillo. The former FBI man, who wired Trujillo's Ciudad Trujillo offices for sound, received a minimum prison sentence of eight months for not identifying himself as in the pay of a foreign government. While the Ernst report overlooked or discounted the documentary evidence linking Murphy with Galindez, it tried to prove that Murphy's flight from Florida, with the mysterious passenger, must have been to Cuba rather than to the Dominican Republic. Not enough time elapsed between the time the plane left Lantana field and returned to Tamiami to allow it to make the seven-hour flight to Monte Cristi Airport, refuel, and return. The witness who had told the Ernst investigators that Murphy returned to Tamiami at 3:00

P.M., upon further questioning said he had made a mistake. Sidney Stein, co-owner of the Blue Star Aviation Corporation at Tamiami Airport changed his story to set the time of Murphy's return to 4:30 or 5:00 P.M., times allowing adequately for the flight, landing, unloading, refueling in the Dominican Republic.

Stories and testimony of hired killers persisted. Rafael (El Muerto, "The Dead One") Soler, Jesus (El Cojo, "The Limping Man") Martinez Jara, a one-eyed bewigged assassin, and "The 42," a military group whose deeds of violence showed that a modern condottieri could be more effective than the mercenaries of the Borgias, were not explained away by the Ernst report.

The Dominican Republic Cultural Association and other public relations agencies of that government continue active in the United States. They serve the interests of Rafael Leonidas Trujillo y Molina, for thirty years dictator of that small Latin American country, which shares half the island of Hispaniola with Haiti. About one-third the size of New York State, the Dominican Republic is an example of autocratic government rare in the world today. It has one legal political party, signed resignations of all appointed officials on file, uncriticized economic and social problems. General Trujillo, a modern dictator, whose annual income is a reputed $40,000,000, seems to follow a formula of success calling for a pound of public relations to an ounce of terror — at least in the United States.

Dominican agents picketed the White House in protest of *Life's* report of the Galindez-Murphy disappearances, and Charles Porter's demands for investigation in Congress. They also picketed Columbia University when Galindez was granted his PhD degree.

Trujillo's legal and public relation representatives in the United States include the most competent with high

connections in the United States government. Franklin
D. Roosevelt, Jr. resigned his agency for Trujillo in New
York, with its $30,000 yearly retainer, as the result of
publicity the press gave the Galindez-Murphy disappearances.

After Galindez was reported missing, the Dominican
Information Agency in New York City issued a memo-
randum stating that he had offered the manuscript of
his book, *The Era of Trujillo,* to Trujillo for $25,000. For
this amount of political blackmail the author would agree
to suppress publication. The arrangements with the
Chilean publishers over a period of months deny this
statement. Only three days before he disappeared, Galindez gave his completed manuscript for the Spanish-
language edition of the book to his publisher's New
York representative. Editorial del Pacifica in Santiago,
Chile, issued the book late in 1956, under the title, *La
Era de Trujillo.* Reported a best seller in Latin America,
the study is evaluated in a professional review as the
"best published systematic analysis of how a dictatorship operates in a Latin American cultural setting." The
planned English edition of *The Era of Trujillo* has been
held up by legal considerations, such as the Public Ad-
ministrator of New York County's determination of the
disposition of the manuscript. Up to this time, the only
available translation of Galindez' report is the excerpts
that have appeared in seven issues of the English edition
of the monthly magazine *Iberica* from September 15,
1956 to March 15, 1957. The whole story of the Galindez-Murphy case seems too fantastic for fiction. If it
is truth, there are many unsolved problems.

Granted that Galindez had paved the way for his death
at the hands of foreign agents, why wasn't he killed in
New York, in the same manner as the previous victims of
asserted Dominican terror? Galindez' friends have said

that he was flown drugged but alive to the Dominican
Republic because Trujillo wished to hold up publication
of the damning expose, *The Era of Trujillo;* that
he wished to discredit Galindez, his arch-critic, by
claiming he had been killed by Communists or was an
embezzler; or that he wished personal revenge for
Galindez' statements imputing the purity of his ancestry
and insulting him and his family by disclosing unsavory
scandals described in pamphlets, in *Bohemia,* a Spanish-language magazine, and included in a satirical novel, *"We Follow on Horseback,"* which the Basque scholar was preparing.

Why were various papers left in Gerald Murphy's
apartment in Ciudad Trujillo showing that he knew Dominican officials and had engaged in activities denied in the official report of his death?

From an examination of the evidence, it seems obvious that all the facts known in the Galindez-Murphy case have not been made public. On the basis of
available reports and documents, it appears that there
may be some relationship between the two disappearances, and that Galindez may have been the passenger
flown from Zahn Airport at Amityville, Long Island to
the Dominican Republic on March 12-13, 1956.

The report of Murphy's death given by the Dominican officials to the United States State Department was
not a true account of Murphy's disappearance and
presumed death, as it contained forged documents, and
left important questions unanswered. This report may
have been an attempt to settle speedily the embarrass-
ing accidental disappearance of an American citizen in
Ciudad Trujillo. In view of related evidence, it appears
more likely that the report was a cover-up for official in-
volvement in the disappearance.

The questions: Where is Dr. Galindez? Where is Gerald Murphy? remain open questions, and investigation of them continues. Only a single article about Jesus de Galindez appeared in the *New York Times* during the year of 1959. It reported a commemoration of the third anniversary of his disappearance, on March 12, 1956.

The United States Justice Department informed Representative Charles Porter on July 10, 1959 that although they had no new developments to report concerning the disappearance of Gerald Murphy, they had a "continuing and untiring interest in solving the case."

The Galindez-Murphy case enigma, the most mysterious disappearances of modern times, remains unsolved.

Further reading:

Hicks, Albert C. Blood in the streets
New York Times. Galindez-Murphy case reviews: December 15, 1957, March 21, 1958, and other issues March 19, 1956 through 1958.
Porter, Charles O. The butcher of the Caribbean *Coronet* 42:50-66 June 1957
Story of a dark international conspiracy *Life* 42:21-31 February 25, 1957
United States asks Dominican Republic to reopen Gerald Murphy case *United States Department of State Bulletin* 36:610-11 April 15, 1957
Varney, Harold L. What is behind the Galindez case *American Mercury* 84:34-42 June 1957

Ambrose Bierce

AMBROSE BIERCE, *right,* with Carrie J. Christiansen, and Walter Neale.

A GRINGO IN EUTHANASIA

Shortly after Ambrose Bierce crossed the border into Mexico at Juarez in December 1913, his death became one of the most famous mysteries of "American Letters." Bierce's writings had given him an international reputation, and his unsolved disappearance added a surprise ending to a controversial career that read like one of his own macabre fables. The legends of Bierce dead are exceeded only by the myths of Bierce living. To one he was "a corpse crying to be buried;" to another, "a gentle, tender-hearted teacher." To others, a prude so conscious of a bare human body that he demanded that two men rowing with him in the covering swiming suits of the early 1900's dive overboard when a woman was sighted in a passing boat. Others found him a libertine, dropped from the Bohemian Club in San Francisco for boasting of his conquests of women. His writing was criticized as hack journalism showing a pedantic illiteracy in over-formal grammar and frequent use of foreign-language phrases. He was praised as a master of the short story and the epigram.

Where Samuel Clemens denied the rumour of his

death, Bierce found it necessary to deny the story that he had never existed. He encouraged the legend that the disabling asthma he suffered from all his life was contracted because he fell asleep on a tombstone while taking an evening walk in a graveyard. Meeting his definition of a cynic, Bierce saw "things as they are, not as they ought to be," and in his terrible vision he found man "worm's meat," and knew the animal that lurked in the heart of each human being.

Bierce's attitude exceeded misanthropy. He not only disliked mankind in a generic, objective way. He disliked each member of the class and recorded his hatred in verbal sketches and comments that are models of satire. Of William Randolph Hearst, his employer for twenty years, he wrote, his voice is "the fragrance of violets made audible." In describing Collis P. Huntington, California railroad tycoon thwarted by Bierce in an attempt to mulct the federal government out of thousands of dollars, Bierce commented, "He says ugly things of the enemy, but he has the tenderness to be careful that they are mostly lies."

Many answers explain the Ambrose Gwinnett Bierce disappearance in his seventy-first year. He died of hardship crossing the plains of Sonora, Mexico with the revolutionist Pancho Villa. He was shot by Villa after criticizing him. He was killed trying to join Carranza's army. He died in action, fighting with the Villa forces at the siege of Ojinaga. He was killed at Torreon. He was murdered in Mexico for the $2000 gold he carried. He spent the last years of his life in a State institution for the mentally ill at Napa, California. He shot himself in a cave-tomb that he had selected in the Grand Canyon of the Colorado.

Is there any one final answer to the riddle of Bierce's death?

"Bitter Bierce" was born in the Northwest Territory of Ohio in 1841. His home was poor, and his first work as a handy man in a brick yard and in a bar-restaurant-grocery and general store. Always deeply resentful of his parents and early life, he referred to his mother and father as "unwashed savages." Lack of formal education and his non-professional work as a boy made him extremely secretive regarding his childhood. He told Walter Neale, his friend and biographer, that he ran away from home when he was sixteen and worked as a reporter on a Chicago newspaper. He really left his parents' house when he enlisted to fight with the Union Army in the Civil War. While his occupation upon entering military service showed as "printer," Bierce's assignments were in topography. He was discharged a full lieutenant, with the reported brevet commission of major, and a war record that commended his leadership qualities.

No part of his life ever replaced the impressions of these war years, when he found "new things under a new sun." Not "all the world was beautiful and strange" with an "element of enchantment," as he later wrote of the battle scenes. There were scenes of disaster and injury that make his collection of Civil War stories, *In the Midst of Life,* as terrible an indictment of war as has ever been written. The glades of silent, bleeding crawling men moving with a senseless animal tropism toward water must have been seen, as described with horrible casualness in *Chicamauga.*

Perhaps it was from this controlled cruelty and planned murder of his military service that death became his familiar. After the war, he lived for several years on the west coast, and wrote articles and columns, more as an avocation, while he earned his living as a nightwatchman and other work in the United States mint. For several years he lived in England working as a journalist, and upon his return to Oakland, Bierce began his work for William Randolph Hearst, writing a weekly column for the San Francisco *Examiner*.

Separated from his wife for many years before they were finally divorced only weeks before her death, Bierce saw his two sons die under tragic conditions. One was shot in a brawl over a girl, the other's death was caused by excessive drinking. During the later years of his life, Bierce lived alone in Washington, D.C. A small income from investments, from book royalties, story reprint rights, and articles, and his Civil War pension allowed him to live modestly and to travel in the United States. For several years he edited his *Collected Works,* and when, in 1909, the volumes were finished, Bierce felt the increasing burden of age. Whenever he returned to San Francisco, his home for many years, he found the friends and the writers he had helped as students dispersed and with changed interests. Two or three times he walked again over the battlefields of the Civil War — Chicamauga, Shiloh, Kenesaw Mountain, where he fought fifty-one years before. His nostalgic letters urged a friend to view the wooded hills and the "purple valleys full of sleep" in the "hazy season."

Extreme attacks of asthma that always bothered Bierce and the disabilities of age made him a semi-invalid. His friends knew of the choking and coughing spells that racked him in his rooms in Washington and on trains and in hotels at stopping points on his now infrequent travels. He found it increasingly difficult to leave the calm and comfort of his easy chair.

Late in 1913, Bierce told friends and reporters that he was going to Mexico. He spoke of a journey by horseback through Mexico, down South America and on foot and muleback from Santiago, Chile over the Andes to Buenos

Aires, and then to England, where he first became famous as a journalist and author in the five years from
1872-1877.

The fiction of this story should be obvious, considering
that he was seventy-one years of age, had not been on a
horse for thirty years, and had continual severe asthmat-
ic attacks that made him disinclined to travel. He had
shown no previous interest in Central and South America, and had been scathing in his criticism of Pancho
Villa, Mexican revolutionary leader. Bierce even
cautioned his friends not to believe everything the
newspapers said of the purpose of his journey. "After
all," he confessed, "I had to tell them something."

Evidence does show, however, that this proposed journey was carefully planned and arranged with finality.
There were farewell letters, written during the prepa-
rations for departure on his journey, when he warned
that he did not except to come back and that nobody
would find his bones. "My work is finished and so am
I," he wrote. "If you hear of my being stood up against
a Mexican stone wall and shot to rags please know that
I think that a pretty good way to depart this life. It beats
old age, disease and falling down the cellar stairs." He
confided that he was "sleepy for death," and "dressed
for death." He referred to his trip as his "Jornanda del
muerto," journey of death.

He had followed the newspaper articles on the fierce
fighting in Mexico between the forces of rebel Pancho
Villa and Victoriano Huerto, who had made himself
president by the assassination of president Francisco
Madero. Considering the stories of Mexican disregard of
American life and property across the border, Bierce
commented, "To be a Gringo in Mexico, that is indeed
euthanasia."

No forwarding address was left for sending on of the

mail he received at the Army and Navy Club in Washington, and Bierce instructed them to return unopened all letters. If the sender was not identified, he asked the Club to give the letter to the postman, marked "unclaimed."

In addition to the letters, there was Bierce's life-long dislike of the trappings of death. He had made fun of contemporary burial practices, and had never allowed any marker to be placed on the graves of his wife or children. His friend Neale said Bierce wished "to crawl off into some cave and die like a free beast," when death approached.

Then, too, there was his public defense of suicide and his privately expressed intention to do away with himself before he became senile — "at about seventy." Walter Neale, Bierce's most frequent companion in the years preceding his disappearance, tells in his biography of Bierce that the writer took on his journey a revolver brought to him from Germany by a friend. In the summer of 1912, the previous year, he said that Bierce had visited the Grand Canyon of the Colorado, and on his return to Washington had shown him a photograph of the spot he had picked for his "last earthly habitat."

Contrary to reports that Bierce carried $2000 in gold, Neale says he had only enough money to get to Chihuahua, and had made no arrangement for additional funds to be sent to him. Miss Carrie Christiansen, Bierce's friend for several years in Washington, did send him one or more royalty checks according to the record she kept of Bierce's frequent letters to her after he left on his trip.

Several months before he left Washington, Bierce asked Neale to prepare assignments of all his possessions and financial interests, including copyrights, royalties and republication rights, to Miss Christiansen. This Neale did in September 1913. Bierce made a further disposition of his possessions by making a gift of $500 to the infant daughter of some friends. He wrote to his daughter describing his only other literary property, a biography he was completing. When he finished the book, during his journey, one of his letters gave instructions for getting the trunk containing the manuscript from a hotel in Laredo. The trunk and manuscript were never found.

During the first weeks of his trip, Bierce's letters to Miss Christiansen, to his daughter and friends record the progress of his Journey. He visited again the "Enchanted Forest" of the Civil War battlefields. He was interviewed for a news article in New Orleans. He visited Galveston, San Antonio, Laredo. It was from Juarez that he wrote to his daughter, Helen, telling her that he left his trunk, with the completed biography he had been working on, in Laredo, before he crossed into Mexico.

His last letters postmarked Chihuahua, Mexico were mailed near Christmas 1913. The final correspondence, post-marked Chihuahua, December 26, 1913, told of his plan to go to Ojinaga with the Villa army as an observer. No trace of Ambrose Bierce was ever found after this letter. Investigations followed his journey to the border, but relatives, friends, journalists, the United States State Department and War Department, and Pinkerton detectives found no clues as to where he went or what happened to him after the letter mailed in Chihuahua the day after Christmas in 1913. There were rumors that he had been killed in action at the siege of Ojinaga. Carey McWilliams, biographer of Bierce, accepts this explanation. Another explanation of his vanishing is that Villa had Bierce shot because he insulted the Mexican leader after drinking too much. Mexicans, and some Americans, recalled "a tall American" in the area, but there was never any proof it was Bierce.

Newspaper reporter George F. Weeks, an old friend of Bierce, went to Mexico in 1919 to find word of the missing writer, believed to be still living somewhere south of the border. Mexicans told Weeks that they had known Bierce. According to their story, he fought with the Villa army, but was executed at the orders of one of Villa's officers, General Tomas Urbina, when he tried to leave the Villa forces to join Venustiana Carranza, carrying him machine guns, near Icamole.

To verify this story, James H. Wilkins, special writer for the San Francisco *Bulletin*, and later mayor of San Rafael, California, went to Mexico the following year. This was seven years after the last word from Bierce. Wilkins' story of Bierce's death, based on the report of a soldier who said he was on the firing squad that shot Bierce near Icamole, appeared in the *Bulletin* of March 24, 1920. The soldier told Wilkins he had removed a picture of the executed man from his pocket, and the news article states that the reporter did not secure the picture and suggests that the soldier destroyed it.

Aside from the letters postmarked Juarez and Chihuahua there is no evidence that Bierce visited or stayed in Mexico. The files of the Passport Office of the United States Department of State disclose no record of a passport in the name of Ambrose Bierce. Complete records of issued passports have been maintained since 1906, but Bierce may have retained his passport issued many years before when he travelled to England, or he may have crossed into Mexico without a passport, as was common practice at the time.

The rumor that Bierce died in Napa State Hospital, a California institution for the insane, is not true, and was based on the fact that Carrie Christiansen, Bierce's friend of many years, returned to Napa, her home town, from Washington after the writer was reported missing.

Walter Neale states that Bierce died by his own hand, and "lies in his niche beside the waters of the Colorado."

H. L. Mencken, who knew Bierce and who reviewed the various theories explaining his disappearance, favors Neale's explanation. From all information about the Bierce mystery, that seems the most logical answer.

However the teller of supernatural tales met his death, he must have died at night, when thin, ghostly mists were rising, the moon half-obscured by a cloud providing fitful light, and a bird cry like a man in terror disturbing the silence.

How these theories, the searches and the years of speculation about his disappearance would have amused Ambrose Bierce. He may have described the unknown as he wrote, "When Death comes cloaked in mystery, he is terrible indeed."

Further reading:

Fatout, Paul. Ambrose Bierce; the devil's lexicographer
McWilliams, Carey. Ambrose Bierce, a biography
McWilliams, Carey. Mystery of Ambrose Bierce. *American Mercury* 22:330-7 March 1931
Mencken, Henry L. Ambrose Bierce mystery *American Mercury* 18:124-6 September 1929
Neale, Walter. Life of Ambrose Bierce
Weeks, George F. The undoubtedly correct account of the fate of Ambrose Bierce *in* California copy, p. 283-93.
Wilson, E. Ambrose Bierce on the Owl Creek Bridge *New Yorker* 28:144-54 December 8, 1951